Andrew Thomas Jaffrey

Hints To Amateur Gardeners

Andrew Thomas Jaffrey

Hints To Amateur Gardeners

ISBN/EAN: 9783742801579

Manufactured in Europe, USA, Canada, Australia, Japa

Cover: Foto ©Lupo / pixelio.de

Manufactured and distributed by brebook publishing software
(www.brebook.com)

Andrew Thomas Jaffrey

Hints To Amateur Gardeners

HINTS

TO

𝕿𝖍𝖊 𝕬𝖒𝖆𝖙𝖊𝖚𝖗 𝕲𝖆𝖗𝖉𝖊𝖓𝖊𝖗𝖘

OF

SOUTHERN INDIA.

BY

ANDREW THOMAS JAFFREY,

LATE SUPDT. OF THE AGRI-HORTICULTURAL SOCIETY'S
BOTANIC GARDENS, MADRAS.

CONTENTS OF THE VOL.

𝕸𝖆𝖉𝖗𝖆𝖘 :
HIGGINBOTHAM AND CO.
1874.

PREFACE.

It is with no small degree of diffidence that I venture to send forth the following Hints to Amateur Gardeners in India. Educated as I have been in the theory of Horticulture in all its branches, and trained in the most approved practice of England, I thought on coming to India that I might without presumption argue to myself as fair a knowledge of the "Art of Gardening" as most of my fellows in similar circumstances. I was not long after arrival in discovering, beyond those points of theory which climate cannot change and a general knowledge of cause and effects, that in regard to practice I had little to boast of, which could be called into action successfully to combat such an *anti-Horticultural climate* if I may so call it as the Carnatic. Two years of experience have however, enabled me to meet the exigencies of this climate, and to obtain a measure of success in Gardening operations, which I hope will warrant my humble endeavours to advance the cause of Horticulture. I have no other object in view, and if these "Hints" are favourably received, I trust to be able to add to their *number*, from time to time, as leisure and opportunity permit.

HORTICULTURAL GARDENS,
    December 1855.

SEEDS.

In giving orders for seeds, whether of Vegetables or Flowers, too much attention cannot be paid to conveying proper instruction to your agent or Seeds-man as regards their age. They are required in the "Carnatic" from the beginning of August till December, for successive sowings, and to meet failures arising from climatic uncertainties and other causes, to be treated on hereafter. As to the possibility of obtaining any great variety of the current year's growth, it is almost out of the question. All who know the climate of England must be aware that the majority of seeds are ripened in autumn, and do not find their way into the merchant's hands in time for that year's supply. The majority of seed merchants have generally on hand one year's supply of such seeds as keep well, to enable them to meet failures which often occur; orders fulfilled from this reserve stock might succeed, but the seeds are not so desirable for India as from the *fresh* supply. There is another *thing* under this head often overlooked, viz., the choice of merchants. Deal with men of the best repute, and if they deal with you, reward them with early remittance, or you cannot expect they will care long for, or faithfully administer to your wants.

MODE OF TESTING.

Many and various have been the suggestions to overcome this difficulty; the best and most efficient is to sow a few seeds of each packet in small flower pots, counting them as put in and doing the same after germination,—this is a process that requires time, and should be done with great care and attention as to varieties, delaying as short a time after their arrival as possible. Another plan is that of subjecting them to the test of water; based as the principle is upon liquids, and solids, volume, and weight, it seldom fails to prove the quality of the majority of seeds excepting those whose buoyant appendages are greater in size than the seed itself, for instance carrots, parsnips, &c. There are some seeds that contain air within the kernel, and a large quantity of oil, whose state cannot be proven by such test. The plan to be adopted in thus testing the majority of seeds, is to take a tumbler of water into which throw a small quantity, a pinch betwixt the finger and thumb is sufficient; the good seeds immediately descend displacing their own volume of water, while the bad swim on the top; some descend half way and linger there a few moments, but invariably return to the surface. If parties, who are in the habit of sending seeds to England, or elsewhere, would adopt this test, carefully drying the seeds afterwards, much useless expense to themselves and disappointment to their Correspondents would be saved; as in many cases Indian seeds, though plump and fresh to the eye, when taken from the plant, will be found useless.

PRESERVATION OF.

As the showers usually occur in July, and continue at intervals till the North East monsoon sets in, care must be taken to preserve from damp all imported seeds, but especially the smaller varieties. If not immediately sown, the simplest plan is to roll the packets up in a piece of flannel or woollen cloth, and place them in a close shutting drawer or almirah; those who receive seeds and carelessly throw them aside until wanted, have only themselves to blame if germination does not take place. The complaints against the seeds sent to India are like those against the weather, " What a bad season, &c., and what bad seeds we have had," while careless exposure of seeds for a few days often proves their destruction. Those who are in the habit of preserving Indian seeds to send to England or elsewhere, should bear in mind that the labor of gathering and putting them into paper bags does not give any practical proof that they are really good. A few hints on preparation of Indian seeds therefore may not be out of place here. All seeds, with anything like a fleshy substance surrounding them, should, when gathered, if ripe, be deprived of it by clean-washing in water and then be perfectly dried, some will not part with their covering by washing, being of a very glutinous nature; to clean such, mix them up in fine sand, and dry, after which they will become perfectly clean by slight friction between the hands, and may then be separated from the sand. There are other varieties of seeds very plentiful in India not un-like small berries, those if only partially dried, and packed amongst others, often destroy the whole lot; such berries ought to be opened and the seeds cleaned. To sum up the whole in a few words, let all the seeds taken from such as are called flowering plants in India be cleaned to the shell of each individual seed, and be made perfectly free from damp before packing. In collecting seeds by all means choose them from the healthiest plants if obtainable.

SOIL ADAPTED FOR SOWING OF.

It is a matter of regret that the soils on the plains of India are in general of such a nature that they cannot be converted into a state fit for horticultural operations, unless at a great expense. A simple and generally available compost can be made with the following ingredients, at least in the neigh-bourhood of Madras. Take six cart-loads of decayed horse manure, ten of red earth, and ten of decayed vegetable matter. Let the whole be laid up in a square heap, care being taken to put them in repeated layers first red earth, then horse manure, next vegetable matter, repeating it thus till the whole is finished. It would be found of great advantage to sprinkle two or three handsful of powdered lime upon each layer of vegetable mould. After the soils are collected in a heap, put above all a good layer of fresh bullocks' manure so arranged as to retain water from running down the sides of the heap, and then water the whole from the top till well soaked, when it must be allowed to stand for four or five weeks, after which it ought to be turned and well mixed together, using the precaution to remove any *bullock* manure still remaining on the top before commencing. In two weeks more, the soil will be fit for use, when it should be put in a covered place to preserve it from the heavy rains which would render it almost useless : (a well built cistern into which the various soils mentioned above might be put and then filled with water would make a preferable soil, but on a more expensive scale.) The soil given here answers equally well for raising seeds or the pot culture of plants in general ; adding sand to the soil for sowing seeds or potting plants, is not usually found to suit unless predominating for horticultural operations in Madras. The heat engendered in the soil is bad enough without adding ingredients essentially tending to make it worse, the best way to create porosity in the soil is to introduce some pieces of charcoal, broken bricks or stones. The successful growth of plants depends much (when placed in an artificial position as they must be in pots) upon a free circulation of air in the soil.

SOWING OF.

In consequence of the heavy rains that generally prevail during the seed time in Madras, the majority of seeds are sown in pots which though probably not generally known, is the most difficult way of raising seeds with inexperienced and careless cultivators, as Indian gardeners really are.

9

The following directions may prove of some value to the Indian Amateur. The first thing to be considered after soil, is the flower pots. Let them be well perforated with holes in and around the bottom, giving thereby perfect drainage and air, to aid which let there be put in at least four inches of broken pots or bricks carefully arranged so as to prevent the soil from falling through them ; to make doubly sure this will not take place, spread over the drainage a handful of dry leaves, before the soil is put in. The condition of the soil to be used is of the most material consideration, it should be examined some days beforehand, and if found too dry it ought to be watered with tank water, in order to create a moisture sufficient to excite vegetation. The reason for this will be given under the head of watering. When the soil is in a state fit to be used, which will be in two days, if too much water has not been applied (the *if* in this instance refers particularly to Native gardeners, who require careful watching on this head) and those who really wish to succeed must make up their minds to look after it themselves. There are few in Madras who are not aware of Mrs. E. Elliot's success in Floriculture ; that lady wrought no miracles ; her success arose in a great measure from individual care and attention. Amateur gardening no doubt is an expensive amusement, but it will be far less costly to those who will give their personal supervision with unwearied perseverance. Let pots (or *drained boxes) be filled to within one inch of the top, not packing too firmly, levelling well and removing all irregularities in the shape of stones, &c. ; have a bamboo sieve at hand, through which sift some soil, laying about half an inch upon the surface of that already in the pots, let this likewise be levelled, after which press the whole surface gently with something flat ; a circular

' Boxes 6 or 8 inches deep with holes in their bottoms are preferable to pots.

B

piece of wood with a handle rising from the middle is best. The reason for pressing the soil is to prevent the seeds from sinking on the application of water; if this precaution be not taken, they may find their way to the middle of the pots, and in consequence cannot be expected to vegetate. The next thing is to sow the seeds regularly over the prepared surface, and cover it with fine sifted soil, again pressing it very gently; covering in the seed.* Nothing can be so destructive to seeds as an overcovering of soil; the usual rule, in this matter, is to cover to the depth of the seed themselves, and if they are very small no earth covering is required, merely press them gently into the soil and cover with a pane of glass till they germinate, when the glass should be gradually raised, during three or four days, after which it may be removed. The best time to sow seeds is after the atmosphere has been somewhat cooled and moistened by a good fall of rain, when they may be sown successively if required, every week or ten days till about Christmas. I am not prepared at present to give a calendar at all trustworthy which would meet the wants of residents in the various climates of Southern India, but there would be little difficulty in its compilation when once furnished with the requisite data, viz., when the rains commence, how long they continue, the average heat during the cold months, and their duration throughout the various districts.

WATERING OF.

Seeds, and especially such as have travelled a great distance should not receive any water for at least 12 hours after they are sown, in very damp weather they may stand 48 (see Soil.) Germination will be excited by the moisture of the soil in which they are sown; more injury is done by the indiscriminate use of water (throughout horticulture) than

---

* A point requiring especial attention and care, according to their size.

perhaps by any other means, and this is not confined to Indian gardeners. It must be borne in mind that an undue amount of water creates rapid excitement in seeds, more especially in a tropical climate, and causes them to germinate before they are prepared (after to complete a drying) to perpetuate their existence, according to the laws of nature. A gentle and gradual excitement is therefore perferable to enable the embryo plant, which may be an exotic, gradually to develop itself into life ; another important item is the temperature of the water to be applied ; this is a point upon which a great want of knowledge usually prevails, but it is of material importance. How often are plants of the most delicate nature watered from wells ; nothing is more injurious to a prospect of success ; well water is usually too cold, nor is the cold the only detriment, for it will in most cases be found hard, and as such, containing ingredients prejudicial to vegetation in general. If any one wishes to prove this, let him water radishes with hard water, and the result will be a hard fibrous root. Let him try the same upon water cresses, essentially a hard water plant, and he will get an excellent crop. Here is an exception to the general rule. Seeds and plants in general ought to be irrigated with water, which has been exposed to the sun in tanks or cisterns for at least one day, when it will be found to have undergone favourable chemical changes, and have become of a temperature nearly assimilating to that of the soil ; if applied in the evening, these conditions are still more absolutely necessary to prevent the plants from receiving a check. Watering seeds ought to be done with watering pots, the nozzles of which are perforated with minute holes, so as to admit of the water falling gently from them upon the soil ; much should not be applied till germination takes place and the plants have formed leaves, when care must be used that the seedlings do not get wet and dry alternately, for if such takes place they will be found to drop off one by one, rotting at the neck close to the soil. To overcome this, a gentle and continued moisture is necessary with sufficiency of light, without sun, until the plants have formed proper leaves to enable them to bring into action their various functions. There may be a deal of trouble in attending to all these details, yet they are requisite towards obtaining even a small degree of success in a country where gardening is in reality a mountain of difficulties.

INSECTS, DESTRUCTIVE OF, AFTER SOWING.

The enemies of gardening in India in the shape of insects are innumerable. The most destructive to seeds is the small red ant, which sometimes carries off a whole sowing in a few hours. There are many ways to entrap this depredator if he appear in moderate numbers, but so vast are the armies, and so persevering are their efforts, that nothing can overcome them but surrounding the pot or boxes with water. This can be accomplished by getting some shallow seed pans made large enough to invert pots in their inside, upon which should be placed the pots, &c., containing the seeds, filling the flat pans with water, and keeping them so till all danger of their being carried away is past.

WATERING PLANTS.

No point in Horticulture commands a position of such importance as this, nor is there any part of the practical treatment of plants requiring more knowledge on the part of the cultivators; plants that are grown in pots depend in a great measure upon hand watering, such being the case, an intimate acquitance with the character of the plants to which water is applied is requisite. Amateurs who cultivate a few flowers for their own amusement, seldom allow them to suffer for the want of water, but the mischief in nine cases out of ten arises from giving them too great a supply: more plants are killed and disfigured by too much water than anything else. When plants become sickly and look as if they would quar-

rel with each other about the poverty of their appearance, too
much water is generally the cause coupled with imperfect
drainage; the usual antidote, however, is to give them more;
death inevitably follows, and the climate gets the blame.
No doubt climate has something to do with plants becoming
sickly, but the want of skill and attention on the part of the
gardeners is the principal cause of their unhealthy condition.
The first thing that ought to occupy the attention of individuals who intend to cultivate plants, whether as amateurs or
for the purpose of establishing a public institution, is to secure
a plentiful supply of water and that of the best quality, viz.,
"soft water," or what may be termed, water containing
earthly salts; all oxides, or salts of iron, are injurious to
vegetation. The next subject for consideration is its temperature, which should be equal to that of the soil if possible. If too cold, it checks the plants, and anomalous as it
may appear, if too warm, the same effects ensue. The injury arising from the application of cold water is done at the
time; the warm fluid produces a rapid evaporation and causes
a chill more detrimental in its effects than the other. Water
should not be applied while the sun's rays are upon the
plants, the evening is decidedly the best time, taking for
granted that the water to be used has been exposed to the
sun a whole day. I am perfectly unaware, after two years
close observation of the Native gardeners, of any rule or
system upon which they conduct this important process of
Horticulture, probably it is a " time-sanctioned" practice,
either drown or starve, there is no medium, and it will continue to be so till an end is put to watering plants with
earthen pots. This system is entirely opposed to nature, all
gardens therefore should be well supplied with watering
pots of all sizes, properly constructed. Under the present
system of watering, the soil in the pots betwixt washing and
evaporation, cannot be fit to sustain healthy life in plants, nor
is this all, the undue pressure caused by such heavy water-

ing renders the soil in a great measure impervious to air, when a free circulation ought invariably to exist. To give instructions as to when water ought to be applied is out of the question, experience must be learned from personal observation. In this climate, there is no general rule, in many cases instead of plants enjoying a season of excitement succeeded by one of repose, the latter is entirely wanting and the excitement is continued until the plant may be fairly said to destroy itself by its own unnatural exertions. In these cases, flowers continue to be produced, gradually diminishing in size, and the whole plant appears to be shrinking into nothing, till finally it becomes a perfect wreck, totally incapable of any successful treatment. The exciting influence of a Tropical climate has unquestionably much to do with this, but the mischief is aided by the plant being artificially stimulated out of season, instead of every endeavour being made to give repose after a season of excitement and the same time retain healthy life. To create at all seasons an artificial atmosphere, adapted to the cultivation of plants from the various regions of the globe, would be a matter of the utmost difficulty, and perhaps an impossibility on the plains of India. The hot winds, so far as I have as yet experienced, put an end to all speculations of a practical nature upon such a subject. In climates, where danger to plants arising from cold is apprehended, rather than heat, the difficulty is easily got over, but the formation of a temperature equal to about summer heat in the midst of a surrounding atmosphere of some 120 or 130 degrees, has not, I believe, yet been obtained, and is, I fear, as mentioned above, almost an impossibility.

REGISTERED COPYRIGHT.

HINTS

TO

𝕿𝖍𝖊 𝕬𝖒𝖆𝖙𝖊𝖚𝖗 𝕲𝖆𝖗𝖉𝖊𝖓𝖊𝖗𝖘

OF

SOUTHERN INDIA.

BY

ANDREW THOMAS JAFFREY,

SUPERINTENDENT OF THE AGRI-HORTICULTURAL SOCIETY'S
BOTANIC GARDENS, MADRAS.

' What is worth doing at all, is worth doing well."

No. 2.

FLORA DOMESTICA.

MADRAS:

RE-PRINTED AT THE ASYLUM PRESS, MOUNT ROAD,
BY WILLIAM THOMAS.
1868.

Annuals.—By this name all plants are designated that flower, perfect their seeds and perish in the same season.

Biennials—Are plants that require two years to develop their growth and then decay.

Perennials.—Plants growing for many seasons and flowering annually, their roots remain alive for a series of years. Perennials have herbaceous stems which continue yearly to flower and decay.

The division of the plants into annuals, biennials, and perennials, is according to the duration of their roots, however, this varies under climatic influences. A plant considered annual in a northern climate, is in many cases biennial or even perennial in the tropics, on the other hand perennials of the tropics often become annuals in a northern climate.

Indigenous plants.—These are natives of the country, introduced from their wild state into our gardens, either for the beauty of their flowers, or botanical peculiarities.

Exotics.—Plants that have been introduced from other parts of the globe. The greater number of pretty flowers, in Indian gardens, belong to this class, many of which have become acclimatized and grow freely.

Herbaceous plants.—Plants with soft succulent stems or stalks which die to the root every year; of herbaceous plants, some are annual stem and root, some are biennial, existing two years, others perennial existing for many years, by their roots retaining vitality.

Shrubby plants.—These differ from the above in consequence of their ligneous character. A shrub is less than a tree, having several permanent woody stems dividing from the bottom. They are not unlike trees as to their length of duration, but seldom rise higher than twelve feet. They are divided into two classes—Deciduous, and Evergreen. Deciduous are such as lose their foliage entirely at certain seasons. Evergreen retaining the foliage until the new appears, when it gradually falls off.

Colors of Flowers.—The prevailing colors are yellow, scarlet, red, pink, white, orange, blue and purple, varying in tints.

PROPAGATION.

Division of the roots.—A simple mode of increasing a sp. or species, mostly adopted in the case of herbaceous plants. The roots of a growing plant are partly uncovered and a portion or portions carefully removed by the aid of a sharp knife if necessary; the plant operated upon is carefully covered up again, and the severed portions planted and shaded from the sun till they take root.

Suckers.—This name is applied to young shoots, thrown out from the roots of plants, in the vicinity of the stem. They may be successfully removed during the rains with a portion of the root attached and planted. When a tree or shrub has a tendency to throw out suckers, it may safely be inferred that portions of the root will produce young plants if cut into lengths about one inch and a half, and planted horizontally in fine sand one quarter of an inch deep.

Layers.—This is a mode of propagation only necessary in some cases in India, it being useful as a means of increasing plants, that do not strike readily from cuttings. The process is very simple, yet one of great uncertainty with Indian gardeners, this arises from their not using a knife in the operation, it is almost needless to say that a good knife is to the gardener, what the lancet is to the surgeon, invaluable. The operation is conducted as follows : A branch of the tree or shrub to be operated upon is gently bent down to the ground; at the part intended to be inserted in the soil an incision is made, about one inch in length; the knife, which ought to be very sharp, is inserted about one-eighth of an inch below a bud, and gently drawn up, taking care to avoid cutting into the pith or centre of the branch, into the incision made, a small piece of stick should be put to keep it open for the purpose of admitting the soil, then plant two inches deep, taking care to bend the layer down regularly to prevent it from breaking, a little fine sand round the incision is useful, the layer should be carefully pegged to prevent moving about or springing up; if large, it should be tied to a stake. This operation requires patience and a steady hand, it very seldom fails. Passion flowers may be rooted this way in three weeks or a month.

Pipings.—This is a process, generally adopted for the propagation of Pinks, Carnations, and Picotees; the young shoots are pulled off by the hand, the ends cleaned and cut smooth with a sharp knife. The most successful way to treat after being so cleaned is, to put the ends in water for a day before planting; they root very well in boxes or shallow seed pots during the rains, in a soil more approaching to clay than sand.

Cuttings—Will be treated of in a future issue.

CLIMBING PLANTS.

It is not judicious to interfere too much with this class of plants, for the purpose of restraining their young shoots. If they are inclined to grow into an entangled mass they should be thinned out occasionally, but in other respects they succeed best when allowed their liberty. They are the wild denizens of the jungle and will not suffer men to control them with impunity. The true method to manage such a wild nature, is freedom of growth on the one side, and

systematic order on the other. They ought not to be brought
too near a dwelling, nor in any situation frequented by child-
ren or domestics, unless they are kept clear from the ground,
affording as they do, a harbour for snakes when allowed to
accumulate into a mass.

TRELLISES.

This is certainly one of the bad features of domestic
landscape gardening in Madras. Almost every house has its
arched trellis way in front, the object of which I have been
unable to discover? unless it be to perpetuate the advice of
Franklin " learn to stoop." If creepers are introduced into
the garden, in front of the house, they should be placed on
horizontal or globular trellises about 2 feet from the ground,
or made in any form fancy may dictate. If high trellises
are used they should be put as far from the house as possible.

FLOWER-POTS.

The great object of domestic floriculture being to improve
the taste for what is beautiful and ornamental, those who
are interested in such a pursuit ought to endeavour, as much
as possible, to improve the present inelegant shaped flower
pots, in general use. There is no difficulty in doing so,
patterns can be seen any time at the Horticultural Gardens.
The following dimensions will aid as a guide, $3\frac{1}{4}$ inches deep
by $3\frac{1}{2}$ inches wide at the top, $4\frac{1}{2}$ inches deep and $4\frac{1}{2}$ inches
wide at the top, $6\frac{1}{4}$ inches deep and $6\frac{1}{2}$ inches wide at the top,
$8\frac{1}{4}$ inches deep and $8\frac{1}{2}$ inches wide at the top, 12 inches deep
and 12 inches wide at the top, larger sizes to be made upon
the same principle. Seed pans 2 feet wide and 7 inches deep.
The above is inside measurement.

SOILS.

Whatever soil is used in cultivating plants in pots, it
should be prepared some weeks beforehand and ought to be
perfectly free from Vermin.

COMPOSTS.

No. 1. Stable manure, containing a large quantity of the refuse of grass on which horses have been fed, and which generally consists of roots, should be laid up to rot for some time until the roots are dead—then mixed with an equal quantity of red earth and laid by in a shady place for a month, the heap should be watered if the weather is dry. This will make an excellent soil suitable for the majority of Exotics and Indigenous shrubs cultivated in pots, especially Roses, or for renewing flower beds.

No. 2. Decayed leaves and vegetables, generally termed Vegetable Mould. Red earth and well decayed manure in equal parts, with a small sprinkling of lime, will be found well suited for rapid growing plants during the cold months.

No. 3. Fine river sand three parts, vegetable mould one, and decayed manure one part. This compost is well adapted for bulbs in general. Dahlias seem to grow well in it, but require liquid manure occasionally.

LIQUID MANURE.

This is a subject of much importance to Flower cultivators, yet one around which "hangs a doubt" as to the judiciousness of intrusting it to the hands of Native Gardeners. In order to prevent any mistake, adhere to the following directions. Whatever ingredients are used in making the liquid, whether Guano, which is best, or cow manure, never allow it to be applied until perfectly clear. Any deviation from this can be easily detected by the appearance of the manure on the surface of the pots, which will prove highly injurious. Never water plants in pots, with liquid manure, more than once a week.

DRAINAGE.

An important item which must not be overlooked. A good

way to preserve the drainage after the broken bricks or potsherds are put in the bottom of the flower pots (previously perforated with good sized holes,) is to cover them over with coarse river sand, when the flower pots used are of a very large size, then it will be necessary to invert on the top of the drainage a small sized pot; this will tend to admit air, and increase the security of perfect drainage.

Horticultural Division of the Seasons in Madras, &c.

MADRAS.		ENGLAND.
Spring.		*Spring.*
August,		February,
September,	Sow seeds, plant trees and shrubs.	March,
October.		April.
Summer.		*Summer.*
November,		May,
December,	Vegetables should be plentiful	June,
January.		July.
Autumn.		*Autumn.*
February,		August,
March,		September,
April.		October.
Winter.		*Winter.*
May,		November,
June,	Protect tender plants from the hot winds.	December,
July.		January.

A select list of popular Flowers cultivated at Madras.

A.	Antirrhinum.	Bignonia.
Ageratum.	Aphelandra.	Brugmansia.
Aster.	B.	Bulbs.
Allamanda.	Balsam.	C.
Angelone.	Begonia.	Cactus.

Campanula.
Carnation.
Cereus.
Cockscomb.
Collinsia.
Chrysanthemum.
Convolvulous (see
Coreopsis. [Ipomea)

D.

Dahlia.
Daisy.
Delphinium.

E.

Epiphyllum.
Eranthemum.

F.

Fuchsia.

G.

Gardenia.
Geranium.
Gloriosa.

Gloxinia.

H.

Heliotrope.
Hibiscus.
Honeysuckle.
Holyhocks.

I.

Ipomea.

J.

Jasminum.
Juniperus.
Justicia.

L.

Larkspur (see Del-
Lobelia. [phinium)
Lophosphermum.

M.

Marigold.
Maurandya.
Mimosa.
Migoonette.

Myrtle.

N.

Nasturtium.
Nemophila.

O.

Œnothera.

P.

Passiflora.
Pansy.
Petrea
Petunia.
Phlox.
Poivrea.
Portulacea.

T.

Thunbergia.

V.

Verbena.
Violet.

Ageratum cœruleum and Sp. Mexicanum.—Well worth cultivating for its pretty blue flowers, propagated from seed and cuttings, will bloom throughout the year if sheltered from the hot winds, must not be too much shaded, if cultivated in pots use a sandy soil.

Aster, German.—This plant is of so short a duration that it will scarcely remunerate for the trouble taken—to raise it, sow seeds at the commencement of the rains ; when two inches high put them singly into small pots, they will bloom in a few weeks ; require a rich sandy soil.

Allamanda Cathartica.—A pretty climber with showy yellow flowers, propagated by layers or cuttings, too large for pot culture, thrives best when allowed to ramble amongst shrubs ; native of South America.

Angelone grandiflora.—Commonly called Indian Larkspur, a very useful plant for flower borders, easily propagated by cuttings growing in almost any situation, and constantly in flower ; *color blue.*

Antirrhinium majus. Snapdragon.—A native of England, succeeds well during the cold months, seed should be sown during the rains, grows best in a well drained soil not too rich, it often lives through the hot weather, young plants are preferable.

Aphelandra cristata.—A useful shrub either for pot or border cultivation. Flowers orange colored, easily propagated from cuttings in sand, requires a rich soil and plenty of water ; native of West Indies.

Balsams. Balsamina.—This pretty annual, with its various colors, is well worth cultivating in flower beds, requires to be sown thinly in a box or seed pan ; after the *plants* are 2 or 3 inches high they should be transplanted out singly in well manured soil, if to be grown in pots, they should be put in small sized ones at first and re-potted into larger, when requisite, which will be, when the small pots are filled with roots. The soil best adapted for pot culture is, 2 parts strong loam approaching in appearance to brick earth, and 2 parts well decayed manure, with a *little lime,* which will aid in preventing mildew, so destructive to the Balsam, the pots should be well drained and the plants must never be neglected in watering ; said to be a native of the East Indies, on the plains of which country the fine varieties soon degenerate into weeds ; seeds may be sown every month.

Begonia.—Natives of the Tropics, usually found growing on moist rocks, others upon the stems of trees, they require a rich vegetable soil, mixed with pieces of charcoal, propagated from cuttings which require to be kept somewhat dry till they root, and by division of the roots also; seed is very uncertain.

Bignonia, trumpet flower.—There are betwixt 60 and 70 known species and varieties, all of which are trees or shrubby climbers; natives of the tropics growing in any situation or soil; do not succeed well in pots owing to their rapid growth.

Brugmansia candida, white trumpet flower.—This handsome plant requires to be planted out in rich soil and in a situation somewhat shaded from the direct rays of the sun, requires plenty of water, easily propagated from cuttings, during the rains almost any branch will grow; native of Peru.

Bulbs.—Imported bulbs do not succeed well in general, this is owing in a great degree to their being disturbed, the best plan to adopt is to prepare a good piece of ground somewhat raised, to throw off the heavy rains and planting each variety by itself in rows, keeping them clear of weeds. Every season, when they begin to grow, stir up the soil and add a little well decayed horse manure. One thing is perfectly evident regarding this species of plants in India, that the more nursing they receive the weaker they become, they seem to relish neglect, under which they flourish in the greatest beauty. If wanted to be grown in pots, the soil should be three parts sand, and one vegetable mould, and decayed manure. When the bloom appears, a watering of liquid manure once or twice a week will aid them greatly. After the leaves are decayed put them in a dry situation till another season; when they begin to show signs of growth let a slight watering for some time be given to enable them to form new roots, then take out one inch of soil, and put in the same quantity of decayed horse manure mixed with a little sand, after which water freely, till the flowers are past when they should be *gradually dried*.

Cactus.—These plants are a very small division of a large family, they are commonly called melon thistle, and rank amongst botanical curiosities; natives of the tropics; grow in brick and lime rubbish with a little well decayed manure and vegetable mould.

Campanula.—Seldom succeeds in Madras, raised from seeds sown during the rains, the seed requires care, being very small.

Carnations, Dianthus caryophyllus.—These plants succeed pretty well so long as they are kept young, but degenerate soon if not propagated annually, this is done by pipings. The soil in which they are grown must be entirely free from vermin; they succeed well in fine river sand to which has been added to every third part one part of well decayed manure. A beautiful genus of plants embracing about 130 species and varieties, besides a host of florists vars.

Cereus.—This is the largest division of the Cactus family, containing about 147 known species and varieties, a beautiful genus of plants and well worthy the attention of amateurs, there being only two or three species to be found in Madras, easily propagated from cuttings in sand and kept pretty dry, grow well in lime rubbish mixed with vegetable mould or loam and manure, all natives of the tropics.

Cocks-combs.—Little better than weeds in Madras, unless planted in well manured soil and watered with good water, they are not worth pot cultivation, raised from seeds in September and October.

Collinsia.—Seeds of this annual often come to Madras, usefulness very doubtful owing to its tender nature; the general cultivated varieties are natives of California.

Chrysanthemum Indicum. Christmas flowers.—There are many varieties of various colors. If grown in pots they require a good rich soil to which pounded bricks should be added and a little lime to preserve the foliage from mildew to which they are subject. Propagated from division of the roots and cuttings; owing to their succeeding so well in this climate, the introduction of some of the finer varieties from England is worthy of consideration.

Coreopsis, Varieties.—Are annuals well worth cultivating either in pots or the flower garden, raised from seeds, should be sown at various times during the cold months for the purpose of obtaining a succession of bloom, sown in February; they may be had in flower during the hot months, if attended with water, at which season any flower is acceptable.

Dahlia variabilis.—A native of Mexico, the original species were single, the double flowers owe their origin to cultivation. They require a free soil not too rich, owing to the rapid degeneration of the flowers on the plains, they would require to be yearly introduced from England. Ought to be regulated so as to get them in flower after the heavy rains are past, and require to be shaded from the mid-day sun, after flowering, they should be cut down and the roots preserved in pots of sand in a dry place as cool as possible. When they start to grow the following season, if preserved, they should be gently watered for a few days retaining them in the pots of sand, when the shoots are about half an inch long, the roots should be divided with a sharp knife leaving one or two eyes to each division, in a week they may be transplanted into separate pots about 4½ inches wide, after the pots are filled with roots they should be repotted into pots in which they are intended to flower; after growing some size let them be neatly staked, taking care not to injure the roots.

Daisy, Bellis perennis.—This plant and its varieties seldom live through the hot season, and do not remunerate for the trouble taken to raise them, unless required as a "Souvenir".

of home. Easily raised from seeds sown during the rains. Natives of Britain and Italy.

Delphinium, Larkspur.—Succeeds well from Hyderabad seed. Should be sown thinly in middling sized pots, where they ought to be allowed to flower. If too thick when two inches high, thin them out until they are about 2½ inches apart. The annual varieties are natives of Switzerland and England ; require a somewhat rich soil.

Epiphyllum.—This is another division of the Cactus family, containing about 20 known species and varieties. Beautiful plants with flat succulent jointed leaves, from the ends of which the flowers proceed. Grow well in coarse river sand, mixed with pieces of charcoal and a little decayed manure. They require care during the heavy rains, propagated by cuttings, every joint of the leaves will strike in sand. Natives of the tropics.

Eranthemum.—The varieties cultivated in Madras are for the most part indigenous, E. pulchellum and E. montanum, grow in almost any soil and situation. E. bicolor requires shade and plenty of water, only fit for borders and flower beds, propagated by cuttings during the rains.

Fuchsia. Varieties.—It is much to be regretted that this splendid family of plants will not succeed on the plains.

Gardenia radicans, Cape Jasmine.—This favourite shrub is well worth all the care it takes, does little good in pots. Should be planted in a well manured flower bed or border which has been drained with sand, they require a soil more approaching to sand than clay and plenty of water ; propagated by cuttings in boxes or seed pots during the rains. A native of China.

Geraniums.—The varieties of this plant which are worth cultivating, will not endure the heat at Madras. There are a few scented varieties of a coarse nature, but they require little care. Propagated by cuttings, which ought to be kept somewhat dry till they root.

Gloriosa.—See Bulbs.

Gloxinia.—The varieties found at Madras are G. maculata and G. caulescens. Both succeed very well, if the roots are started into growth at the commencement of the rains. They require a rich soil well drained. G. caulescens propagated by leaves under glass. G. maculata by division of the roots, require treatment similar to dahlias for the preservation of the roots, they should not be grown in too large pots.

Heliotrope, H. Peruvianum.—Should be grown in a soil more approaching to sand than clay, easily cultivated in pots, or the flower beds, propagated by cuttings in sand under glass. They require to be protected from the hot winds.

Hibiscus, Shoe flower.—In general showy shrubs with various colored flowers. Well adapted for shrubberries, require pruning occasionally to keep them in form, &c. There are more than 80 known species and varieties, all natives of the tropics. Propagated by cuttings and seed during the cold weather.

Holyhocks, Althea rosea.—Varieties.—Well worth cultivating on the plains during the cold months. Seeds should be sown thinly in wooden boxes successively during the rains. When they have found 3 or 4 leaves they should be planted out in the flower garden. Nothing can excel their gaudy appearance, if planted in well prepared soil, where they will grow from 6 to 12 feet high.. Owing to their rapid development, it is a doubtful matter if double flowers will ever be had on the plains. They take about six weeks or two months from the time of sowing to flowering. Native of China.

Honeysuckle, Caprifolium.—This genera is seldom to be found on the plains in a very satisfactory condition, with few exceptions, they are generally natives of cold countries, requiring rich vegetable soil, grow freely from cuttings under glass if not kept too damp.

Ipomea.—Species and varieties, pretty creepers flowering in the morning. They greatly enhance the beauty of Indian gardens, when the various colors are well arranged, raised from seeds sown at the commencement of the rains, they may be sown where intended to flower. Any garden soil will suit, if not too heavy. .

Jasminum.—Very pretty shrubs with white and yellow flowers, in most cases scented, the yellow varieties should be grown in pots, being native of the higher latitudes of the tropics, often perish during the hot season, they require a loamy soil well manured, and perfect drainage. The white varieties grow well in the flower borders, requiring to be pruned occasionally, to keep them in proper form, this should be done after flowering.

Juniperus.—Does well in certain situations on the plains, ought to be planted where drainage can be had and protection from the mid-day sun if possible, requires plenty of water during the hot season, propagated by seeds and layers, seedlings preferred.

Justicia.—For the most part shrubs growing in any situation and soil.

Larkspur.—See Delphinium.

Lavender.—Requires pot culture and careful renewing of the stock every season by cuttings, old plants being very uncertain ; should be planted in rather poor soil. Seeds sown at the commencement of the rains. Native of the South of Europe.

Lobelia Erinus.— Varieties.— Pretty little procumbent plants, generally having blue flowers, succeed well in the flower beds, raised from seeds. Will not live through the hot weather.

Lophospermum, Scandens and Hendersonii.—Herbaceous climbing plants with pink bell flowers, raised from seeds and cuttings, require a sandy soil, or they will not flower freely. Natives of Mexico.

Marigold, Tagetes patula and erecta.—Any of the species will do well on the plains, they require to be sown thinly in boxes or pots during the rains, when two or three inches high, they should be transplanted into the flower beds, called French and African Marigolds.

Maurandya Barclayana, &c.—Very pretty creepers, with pink, white and blue flowers, require a rich soil, well adapted for mixing amongst other creepers on arbors or trellises.

Mimosa, Sensitive plant.—This vegetable wonder will grow in almost any situation and soil, raised easily from seeds.

Mignonette, Reseda odorata.—A general favorite in all countries, may be had in great luxuriance on the plains during the cold months, does not like to be transplanted, and ought invariably whether in pots or flowers beds to be sown where intended to flower, requires an open soil and free drainage, sometimes lives through the hot season if sheltered by a high building.

Myrtle, Myrtus communis, &c.—A well known favorite, succeeds best in the flower borders, propagated by cuttings in sand under glass.

Nasturtium.—Indian cress. *Tropæolam majus* and *minus*, raised from seeds sown at the commencement of the rains, succeeds well if not too much exposed to the sun, of easy cultivation, seldom produces seed on the plains, the introduction of the other species and varieties cannot be recommended. Natives of Peru.

Nemophila insignis and *maculata.*—Pretty annuals, too tender to succeed well on the plains, N. maculata the spotted variety succeeds to a certain extent if sown after the heavy rains are past.

Œnothera, Evening Primrose.—There are between 70 and 80 species and varieties of this genera, raised from seeds, cuttings, and layers during the rains, will grow in any good garden soil, succeeds best in the flower beds, requires plenty of water during the hot months, found in various parts of the globe, the majority in North America.

Passion flowers, Passiflora. Varieties.—Beautiful climbers, the greater number of which do well on the plains, they require abundance of water. Not at all adapted for pot culture, easily propagated by cuttings during the rains under glass; some of the common varieties can be propagated in the open air during that season, require a well manured soil. Natives of the Tropics, many of which have been hybridized.

Pansy, Heartsease.—May be raised from seed sown at the commencement of the rains, will hardly repay the trouble.

Petrea volubilis.—Is a beautiful creeper with blue flowers of easy culture, requires exposure to the sun and severe pruning, this should be done at the very commencement of the monsoon, should have plenty of room and good soil, easily propagated by cuttings in the open air during the rains. A Naitve of Vera Cruz.

Petunia. Varieties.—Very useful plants for the flower garden or pots, should be raised from seed at the commencement of the rains, not particular as to soil, but if too rich they do not flower freely, sand three parts and leaf mould and loam one part suit them best. Native of the Tropics.

Phlox, Drummondii and variety *Lepoldina.*—Are useful annuals, succeed well on the plains either in pots or the flower beds, should be sown thinly, and when one or two inches high, transplanted where intended to flower, require in pots a somewhat loamy soil well manured and drained.

Native of Texas, ripens seed freely, which is to be preferred to that imported.

Poivera . coccinea Syn Combretum purpureum.—This at present is the popular favorite amongst climbing plants in Madras ; requires a trellis not too high, the sooner it gets a procumbent position the more luxuriant it will grow and flower, unfit for pot cultivation, easily propagated by cuttings of the young wood in sand under glass. Native of Madagascar.

Poivera grandiflora Syn Combretum grandiflorum.—Similar to the above in habit but having far superior flowers. Native of S. Leone.

Portulacca.—A pretty little succulent annual, opening its flowers in the sun, raised from seed, requires a sandy soil. Native of the Tropics ; requiring little care as regards soil ; should be watered sparingly at all times.

Thunbergia.—Creepers with white, yellow and blue flowers, require a free rich sandy soil and plenty of drainage. The large varieties with blue flowers should be planted out and trained upon pillars, trellises or trees. Natives of the Tropics ; raised from seeds, cuttings, layers, and suckers.

Verbena.—These pretty little flowering plants are too well known to require describing. They do not endure the heat, will require shelter and good drainage during the hot months. Propagated by layers and cuttings.

Violet.—Sweet scented violets. Requires a good rich soil, shelter from the sun and plenty of water, succeed at Madras and flower freely. Plants to be had from the Hills.

HINTS

TO

The Amateur Gardeners

OF

SOUTHERN INDIA.

BY

MR. ANDREW THOMAS JAFFREY.

'What is worth doing at all, is worth doing well."

No. 3.

THE KITCHEN GARDEN.

Fourth Edition Revised.

HIGGINBOTHAM AND CO.
1874.

MADRAS:
PRINTED BY HIGGINBOTHAM AND CO.,
165, MOUNT ROAD.

KITCHEN GARDEN SOIL.

AFTER forming the Garden, laying down walks, &c., the soil whether light, or heavy, should be trenched to the depth of 18 inches, or 2 feet, and thrown up in ridges, at the commencement of the hot weather, so that it may be fully exposed to the influence of the sun, which facilitates pulverization; about a month before the soil so treated is brought under cultivation, the ridges should be levelled, well dug over and any lumps broken, this will be done more easily and effectually after a shower of rain, the surface should be covered to the depth of 6 inches, with decayed vegetable matter, and manure. (The most suitable for vegetable culture is well decayed cow-dung) to which may be added half an inch of ashes, those obtained from burnt animal excrement are best, and lastly, a good sprinkling of air-slacked lime; after which causing the whole to be dug over three times, by so doing the manure will be well incorporated with the soil, then level, lay out in beds, &c.,* ready for plants and seeds.

Kitchen Garden soil will repay the trouble expended upon it if thrown up in ridges every hot season, and much expense be saved as it will always remain in a workable condition, while at the same time vermin will in a great measure be eradicated; ashes should not be applied oftener than every second or third year; as regards manure it stands simply thus " *if you starve your garden, it will starve you in return.*"

A general plan adopted to cure the tenacity of heavy soil, is to add a large volume of sand, and vegetable matter. This plan may be sound enough when circumstances admit of its adoption. But the majority of heavy soils in and

---

* For form of beds see General Remarks.

around Madras, to the depth requisite for cultivation, though considered clayey, are a combination of equal parts, sand, and soluble clay, with scarcely a particle of vegetable matter; such a soil under the influence of heat and water, forms a compact body equal in hardness to sandstone; perfectly impracticable in such a state for Horticultural operations—the reason of this, arises not from the want of a sufficient volume of sand, but from the entire absence of vegetable matter. There can therefore exist no necessity for adding sand of which ingredient there is sufficient, for the requirements of vegetable development.

Whatever soil is intended for Kitchen Gardening, no trouble should be spared in its preparation, such will not only ultimately be a saving of expense; but tend to prevent annual disappointment from bad crops, ravages of insects, &c.

SAND.

Sand though a material element of soil, by itself does not constitute a soil; large tracts of it are found in most parts of India ; and which are looked upon as sterile and unproductive wastes. This character may be true of sand alone—but as sand forms a material and valuable aid in the formation of a good soil, probably much might be done by the judicious application of manure, towards turning what is now deemed unprofitable land into one of value. With a plentiful supply of water, tuberous rooted vegetables will do well in such situations, and the most of vegetables will yield a reasonable crop.

ENGLISH KITCHEN GARDEN VEGETABLES, THEIR CULTIVATION, USES, &C.

For the sake of ready reference the vegetables hereafter mentioned are arranged alphabetically ; being more adapted to the generality of readers than if done according to Systematic Botany—the Botanical and English names are given, while at the same time the uses to which they are applied are added, the varieties which at present are considered suitable to the plains of Southern India, are marked with *Asterisks.*

Alexanders.—Smyrnum olisatrum, and perforatum. The blanched stalks of this perennial herb are used in soups and salads; raised from seed sown in drills, when the seedlings have attained a few perfect leaves, they require to be thinned out to the distance of 12 or 15 inches apart, they will. bear transplanting, and are blanched by the leaf stalks being tied together and earthed up like celery, (which see.)

Angelica.—Angelica Archangelica. Requires to be raised annually from seed, the green stems when young and tender, are used for candies, should be sown in a well prepared bed and thinned when 2 inches high to 1 foot or 18 inches apart.

*Artichoke Jerusalem.—Helianthus tuberosus. Cultivated for the tubers attached to the roots, may be lifted annually, after flowering and kept like potatoes for 3 months, or they may be allowed to remain for years in the same situation, if kept clear of weeds and the ground annually top dressed with manure ; cooked similar to potatoes, and sometimes used as a fricassee.

*Artichoke Garden.—Cynara Scolymus. Little is known of the culture of this plant, flowers are said to have been produced at Madras; but very rarely. For further information see Cardoons.

*Asparagus.—Asparagus officinalis. A very delicate vegetable raised from seed, takes 4 years to come to a proper size for the table, ought not to be cut before the 4th year ; the seedlings when one year old, should be planted in well prepared beds raised 3 inches above the surrounding level ; three years after being transplanted they will produce a crop if the

beds have been annually top dressed with decayed leaves, and
manure. A little salt sprinkled over the beds once a year
during the rains, will be useful to the plants. Native of the sea
coast, a very expensive vegetable to grow in any country.

*Balm.—Mellissa officinalis. Pot herb, young tops and
leaves used in cookery, and dry as tea; raised from seed,
cuttings, &c., all pot herbs should be cut to dry when in
flower, and dried in the shade.

*Basil.—Ocymum Basilicum and minimum. Herbs used
in salads, and soups, raised from seed, require little care in
the culture, almost weeds in Madras.

Beans.—Vicia faba, Windsor beans. Grow freely though
seldom producing fruit, require good light soil, plant in rows
8 inches apart, liable to be destroyed by insects.

*Beans, French.—Phaseolus Sps. and vars. The young
pods used in various culinary purposes, and as pickles
require little care in the culture, the climbing vars. should
be staked like peas.

*Beet.—Beta vulgaris. A well known esculent root, used
in salad, as a pickle, and preserved as a comfiture; the best
are the small varieties; raised from seed, they require a
deep well prepared soil, sown in drills or broad cast, where
intended to grow, when the plants have formed a few leaves,
they ought to be thinned out to about 9 inches apart. Native
of the South of Europe, succeeds well on the plains.

*Beet, white.—Beta cicla. Leaves used in salads; the mid
rib of the leaves as a substitute for Asparagus; treatment
similar to red beet.

Beet Sea.—Beta maritima. Requires a sandy soil; used
as spinach, or a pot herb, raised from seed; of little value.

*Borago.—Borago officinalis. Used as a pot herb, the young
shoots and leaves as salad, required treatment similar to
Angelica, succeeds at Madras, but flowering rather too early

to be of much use ; suitable for the flower garden. Native of England.

Borecole.—Brassica oleracea *var.* Scotch Kale. The winter greens of England and Scotland. Treatment similar to cabbage.

*Brocoli.—Brassica oleracea *var.* Modes of treatment at Madras yet unknown, any further than producing plenty of leaves, which are useful as greens, well worthy of attention, flowers have been produced, requires a rich soil and plenty of water to secure rapid growth ; raised from seed, planted 15 inches apart, probably if grown from cuttings during the rains might be successfully treated.

Burnet.—Poterium Sanguisorbia. Raised from seeds sown annually ; used in salads, of little value as a vegetable.

*Cabbage.—Brassica oleracea *vars.* Nothing is more astonishing, than the wide difference, existing betwixt the cultivated vars. of cabbage, and the original parent ; which is an uninviting weed on the shores of Britain, with wavy green leaves, and yellow flowers like the common mustard. The use to which this vegetable is applied being too well known to require mention ; raised from seeds and cuttings ; requires a free open rich soil and plenty of water ; the surface of the ground round the plants should be repeatedly howed to keep it open and free of weeds, the varieties which seem to grow best at Madras, are the early York, Vanack Nonpariel, Carters matchless, Red, Globe Savoy, Brussels sprouts, and Khnol Koll. The seeds of cabbage should be sown sometime before the commencement of the N. E. Monsoon at Madras, in a well prepared bed not too rich.

*Carrot.—Daucus Carota, and hortensis. Require a deep rich free soil ; succeeds well on the plains, sown broad cast in beds, after the plants have attained some size, they should be thinned out to the distance of 6 inches apart ; used in soups, &c.

Cauliflower.—Brassica oleracea var. An excellent vegetable, but does not flower freely, (see Brocolie.)

Celery.—Apium graveolens. The blanched stalks of this plant forms one of the best salads, and the green leaves are used in soups, succeeds well on the plains under the following treatment. Trenches should be dug 2 feet deep, and 15 inches broad, the earth taken out, thrown up on each side; dig the bottom of the trench well, and put in 9 inches of decayed cow manure and leaves in equal parts, to which add 4 inches of the soil formerly taken out, with a little lime, mix well together and water, in two or three days, plant 9 inches apart. Seed should be sown early in the season, so as to ensure strong plants by the commencement of the rains; at the close of which begin to plant. *To blanch*, when the plants are one foot high they should be earthed up; with the earth on the side of the trenches to the height of 4 inches, the proper way to do this is to take a plant in the left hand, and put the soil round it with the other, taking care not to allow any to get into the heart and not to earth above it, a little lime is required to be dusted about the plants before commencing, it will prevent injury from worms; after the first earthing, the foliage ought never to be watered if possible; as it causes the plant to decay at the centre; the earthing up must be repeated as the plants grow.

Caraway.—Carum Carui. The seeds are used in confectionary, and sometimes as an ingredient in salads. The roots are equal to Parsnips in flavor, of simple growth.

Cardoons.—Cynara Cardunculus. Similar to the garden artichoke; indeed plants of the latter, which grow to a large size might be used as cardoons; in order to prepare this vegetable, the leaves of the artichoke should be cut down, not destroying the heart, at the commencement of the rains, after the young leaves grow to the length of 2 feet, they should be tied together in a bundle, and earthed up like celery, at least

one foot of earth should be raised round the plant, they will
be fit for use in three weeks or a month, raised from seed. The
plants when a good size require to be planted 2 or 3 feet
apart in good soil ; probably this is the only use to which the
garden artichoke could be turned to at Madras.

Chamomille.—Anthemis nobilis and *var.* plena. An aromatic herb, leaves used in garnishing, the flowers as bitters and
fomentations, of easy culture, raised from seed, held in high
estimation, both in popular and scientific " Materia Medica."

Chervil.—Chærophyllum sativum. The leaves are used in
soups and salads. It is worthy of observation that the cultivation of this plant is somewhat dangerous, in consequence of
the close appearance it bears to the common rough Chervil.

Anthriscus vulgaris.—Its cultivation should only be in-
trusted to a professional Gardener, as the latter plant is highly
poisonous, will grow in any common garden soil ; of little
value as a vegetable.

Chives.—Allium Schænoprasum. A *var.* of onion held in
much estimation for its leaves and small bulbs, used in soups
and salads. This vegetable will grow in any common garden soil, requires plenty of water and protection from the ver-
tical rays of the sun, propagated by division of the plants.

Clary.—Salvia Sclarea. An aromatic herb. Wine is made
from the flowers, of easy culture, raised from seed.

Cole-worts.—Brassica oleracea. A *var.* of cabbage, of little
value for the plains, might succeed on the hills, require treatment similar to cabbage.

Coriander.—Coriandrum sativum. An aromatic herb,
young leaves used in curries, seeds for a similar purpose, likewise in confections and decoctions, of easy culture ; raised from
seed, will grow in any good soil.

Cress.—Lepidium sativum, garden cress. Should be sown
broad cast in a bed raised above the level, does little good at
Madras though an excellent ingredient in salads.

Cress.—Nasturtium officinale, water cress. Of easy culture, should be in every garden, requires to be irrigated night and morning direct from a well ; a small bed 2 or 3 yards square, so formed as to be easily irrigated, will produce sufficient for any family during the cold months, the soil near the surface should be somewhat sandy, propagated by seed and division of the plants.

Cress.—American or Bellisle. Has little to recommend, it having a harsh flavour, but owing to its being of a more robust nature than the garden cress, might be easier cultivated on the plains, raised from seed, the young leaves cut when young for salads, requires plenty of water.

Cucumbers.—Cucumis sativus, and *vars*. Said to be an unwholesome vegetable for delicate constitutions, raised from seed which should be two or three years old, sown where intended to fruit, requires a free rich soil. English varieties should be trained on trellises ; when the shoots are 2 feet in length the points should be pinched off to cause them to branch, used in salads and pickles ; sown after the rains are over at Madras, in January, February, and March.

Dill.—Anethum graveolens. Herb leaves used to flavour pickles, the seed as a carminative, and supposed to be used in the manufacture of gin, raised from seed.

Endive.—Cichorium Endiva. Said to be a native of China. Used as salad, has a slight bitter taste, requires treatment similar to lettuce, should be planted on a bed elevated above the level and well manured, when properly grown they average about 15 inches in diameter. Blanched by the leaves being tied together.

Fennel.—Anethum Fœniculum. (See Dill.)

Garlic.—Allium sativum. A *var.* of onion used in curries, soups, &c., propagated by division of the soboliferous bulbs of easy culture in light soil.

Gourd.—Cucurbita *Sps.* and *vars.* A coarse genus of the

cucumber family, generally cultivated throughout the year, of comparative little value as a vegetable, requires rich soil and plenty of room ; it is not commonly known, that the young shoots of all the edible varieties of gourds are an excellent vegetable, used as spinach.

Leeks.—Allium *sp.* This excellent *var.* of the onion tribe is raised from seed sown in boxes or in beds from whence transplanted when 3 or 4 inches high. They can be transplanted into beds 4 inches apart as they grow larger, they require to be earthed up like celery, a few waterings with liquid manure will accelerate their growth.

Lettuce.—Lactuca sativa. Raised from seeds, require a rich soil, no salad is of easier culture than this; English seed generally succeeds best, the Cabbage *vars.* are most suitable for the plains, blanched by tying the leaves together with strands of Plantain narr.

Parsley—Apium Pteroselinum. A well known seasoning herb, used in soups, garnishing, &c., grows well during the cold months, requires a free rich soil, and planted on a bed raised 6 inches above the surface level, raised from seed.

Peas.—Pisum sativum. A well known vegetable. The kinds that grow best at Madras are the Bangalore and Cape seed, sown in drills after the heavy rains are over, the best manure for this vegetable is street sweepings and wood ashes, do little good at Madras after the middle of February. May be sown successively once a fortnight during the cold months. Native country unknown.

Pennyroyal.—Mentha Pulegium. A *var.* of mint used in Cookery as seasoning and in distillation, propagated by division of the plant, like spear mint, requires a rich free soil, plenty of water and shade.

Peppermint.—Mentha piperita. An aromatic herb, raised from seed. This plant might be grown for distillation on the hills, and become a valuable article of commerce, grows freely on the plains.

Potatoes.—Solanum tuberosum. Cultivated for the tubers attached to the roots. Potatoes, cultivated on the plains, are hardly fit for human food in consequence of their never arriving at maturity, they ought to succeed well on the hills ; but wherever grown they will do little good if repeatedly planted on the same spot of ground, they require a change every year, propagated by division of the tuberous roots.

Purslane.—Portulacca sativa and oleracea. Cultivated at one time as a pot herb, now fallen into disuse ; leaves of a succulent nature harmless, tasteless, and inodorus, many *vars.* are cultivated on the plains for their pretty flowers, raised from seed.

*Radish.—Raphanus sativus, radicula, and oblonga. Used in salads, the seed pods when young, make excellent pickles, raised from seed sown thinly on beds broad cast ; require rain water. The red, white, pink and purple turnip *vars.* succeeded best on the plains, the black spanish *R. niger* is of little value, used in salads.

Rape.—Brassica Napus. This plant yields the Rape seed of commerce. Used as salad similar to mustard, the leaves are however eaten when the plant is in seed, of no great value as a vegetable, cultivated like mustard.

Rhubarb.—Rheum, Raphonticum and *vars.* Nothing is known of the culture of this plant at Madras. Used in tarts, and the introduction of good strong roots from England might be tried.

Rocombole.—Allium Scordoprasum. A *sp.* of onion not unlike garlic, used in culinary for the same purpose, said to have a better flavor than its ally ; propagated by seed and bulbs.

*Rosemary, or Dew of the Sea. Rosmarinus officinalis, and *var.* variegata. A medicinal herb ; the leaves yield by distillation a very fragrant essential oil likewise used as tea in cases of headache, requires a well drained soil, propagated by seed and division of the plant.

*Rue.—Ruta graveolens. An evergreen shrub, grows freely in any good soil, used for fowls in the Roup; propagated by cuttings in damp weather.

Sage.—Salvia officinalis. A small shrub, used in culinary for stuffings and flavoring various dishes, difficult to manage, some of the Indian varieties might be more useful.

Salsafy.—Tragopogon Porrifolius. An excellent vegetable cultivated for its white roots which are mild and sweet flavored, requires culture similar to carrots, held in high estimation by the French. The young shoots are sometimes used as Asparagus, which in flavor they resemble a native of England. Raised from seed.

Savory.—Satureja Hortensis and montana. Aromatic herbs now fallen into disuse, used to flavor soups, &c.

Sea Kale.—Crambe Maritima. Cultivation at Madras unknown, and a vegetable not worth experimenting upon.

Shallots.—Allium Ascalonicum. The mildest of the onion tribe, seeds seldom; propagated by the young bulbs, used in sauces, salads, &c.

Sorrel.—Rumex acetosa. Used as spinach and salad, of little value, the French Sorrel, R. scutatus is a very delicate vegetable, of easy culture in light soil.

*Spinach.—Spinacia oleracea. Leaves used as a culinary vegetable, of the easiest culture in rich soil, requires plenty of water, should be sown thinly in drills or broad cast every month or six weeks, may be had during the hot months in sheltered situations, with attention to water.

*Spear mint.—Mentha veridis. Cultivated for the fragrant leaves, which are used in sauces, tea, &c., requires rich soil, shade and plenty of water, propagated by division of the plant.

Spring.—Salad onion. Welsh onion Allium, fistulosum. This onion has little or no bulb, used in soups and salads, may be closely imitated by purchasing a few onions monthly from the bazaar, and planting in any good soil, by this means young onions can always be had for the table.

Sucoory.—Cichorium Intybus. Much used in France as a winter salad under the name of *Barbe du Capucine.* The common way to grow this plant is similar to carrots. When the tapering roots have attained some size, they are lifted, the leaves cut off, the roots are then planted in sand in a dark room or cellar; where in consequence of the absence of light the roots throw out white leaves which make an excellent vegetable. This plant is the Cichory of commerce used in the adulteration of Coffee.

Tansy.—Tanacetum vulgaris and *var.* crispum. The young leaves cut small or used in coloring and flavoring puddings, omlets, cakes, &c. The curled *var.* T. cripsum in garnishing; succeeds on the plains, and grows freely in any good soil.

Tarragon.—Artemisia dracumculus. A salad much used by the French, raised from seed and division of the plant, culture similar to mint.

Thyme.—Thymus vulgaris. An aromatic, perennial, evergreen shrub, raised from seed, requires a sandy soil and free drainage, used in soups, &c.

Tomatoes.—Solanum Lycopersicum and Melogena. A well known vegetable of easy culture, does not require a very rich soil, succeeds best when trained on horizontal trellises, should be thinned occasionally of superfluous shoots, raised from seed, used in sauces, &c.

Turnips.—Brassica Rapa. In general grows indifferently at Madras, requires a free light soil: for growing this vegetable, the manure applied to the soil ought to be kept near the surface, there is one variety, the yellow Maltese worthy of a trial on the plains; raised from seed sown broad cast, when the plants have formed a few leaves they should be thinned to about 6 inches apart; used in soups, stews, &c.

Virginian Poke.—Phytolacca decandra. The young shoots much used in America, and the West Indies as spinach, there is little doubt but that this plant would succeed on the plains of Southern India during the cold months, require a deep rich soil, having large roots, raised from seed, sown annually.

GENERAL REMARKS.

As the cultivation of vegetables on the plains is a work beset with many difficulties, arising from an uncertain climate, ravages of insects, &c., it would be but judicious that such individuals as may be inclined to enter upon it, should do so with discretion, in not attempting to cultivate too large a piece of ground, until they can cultivate a small piece well, by far too little attention is paid to rotation of crops and change of manures, the Native gardeners pay little or no attention to such things, nor are they to be blamed their never being taught them. It is impossible that the same spot of ground can annually yield a good crop of any given plant; the ground that yields a good crop of cabbage one year, will yield good peas the following; it is only by thus changing that healthy produce can be expected. As regards the careful preservation of manure so as to fit it for gardening, or agricultural purposes, it is entirely neglected never being looked after until the very day it is wanted, instead of being on hand months before, so that it might be well made, by being mixed with vegetable matter watered and repeatedly turned over to prevent it from burning. A careless preservation of manure will certainly never tend towards promoting successful Agricultural or Horticultural operations in any country, nor will the continued use of the same kind of manure produce any better results.

The modes adopted in planting vegetables are various, some plant on elevated ridges, other in furrows, and some in beds, the safest and best mode is to lay the ground out in beds 4 feet broad, with a well beaten ridge one foot in breadth along the sides and ends ; it is a saving of space and easily irrigated. Salads, such as lettuce and endive, require beds raised 6 inches above the level and watered with a watering pan, the surface soil of all vegetables should be frequently hoed to keep it open as the water tends to bind it and prevent the access of air. It should likewise be borne in mind that the presence of many trees in a Kitchen Garden are highly detrimental to the growth of the majority of vegetables ; the space occupied by the latter should be as open and free from shade as possible.

HINTS

TO

𝕿𝖍𝖊 𝕬𝖒𝖆𝖙𝖊𝖚𝖗 𝕲𝖆

OF

SOUTHERN INDIA.

BY

ANDREW THOMAS JAFFREY,

SUPERINTENDENT OF THE AGRI-HORTICULTURAL SOCIETY'S BOTANIC
GARDENS, MADRAS.

"He who waits for an opportunity to do much at once, may breathe out his
life on idle wishes, and regret in the last hour his useless intentions
and barren zeal."

No. 4.

INDIAN VEGETABLES.

SECOND EDITION.

MADRAS:
HIGGINBOTHAM AND CO.

1872.

PRINTED BY HIGGINBOTHAM AND CO., MOUNT ROAD, MADRAS—JUNE 1872.

INDIAN VEGETABLES.

In commencing to collect materials for the present issue, I had not the slightest idea that my enquiries would be attended with so much difficulty, but being in a great measure without a guide, it required much painstaking to make the present number as complete a compendium as possible ; with all the care taken this issue is somewhat incomplete, for so manifold and often obscure are the varieties of vegetables growing by the way side in India, that it would require a greater amount of leisure than I possess, to search through the wide spread distribution of vegetable-life, to discover the correct Botanical nomenclature of all the plants used as pot herbs in this country ; however, it is hoped, that this pamphlet, will lay a foundation for those who may be inclined to prosecute the enquiries to a greater length ; it has no doubt seemed a great mystery to many how the poorer class of natives contrive to subsist on their small incomes, this is in some measure explained, when the hedges and ditches are found to teem with wholesome esculents, many of which are cultivated by the Market Gardeners. The cultivation of not a few varieties of these indigenous vegetables seems worthy of attention ; as it is chiefly by the use of them that the masses obtain a scanty supply during the hot months, while, at the same time, their cultivation is attended with very little difficulty. The arrangement now adopted is similar to that of the former numbers of the series, (Alphabetical), the Botanical and Tamil names being given with a brief description of the plants, their appearance, uses, &c., those about which any doubt existed have been omitted, and such as may be considered useful to the European community are marked with asterisks. The subject of vegetable culture being one of much importance to India, it will be continued in No. 5.

* Abelmoschus esculentus. *Benday-kai, Tamil.*—The seed pods of this plant when young are an excellent esculent, generally cultivated ; when grown in rich soil, they are considerably improved in quality.

Achryanthes aspera. *Naihooroove-keeray,* T.—This is a common weed with flowers in rough terminal spikes, seldom eaten alone, and in general used in what is called by the natives Calavay-keeray (mixed greens.)

Æschynomene aspera. *Sudday-keeray,* T.—A herbaceous perennial, usually found by the sides of tanks, &c., stems spongy, the leaflets are used as greens.

Agati grandiflora, Var alba.—*Agati-keeray Poo,* &c., T.—The leaves and flowers of this tree are used in soups, and as greens, the pods are sometimes eaten, though seldom. This tree is much cultivated, (being of rapid growth) in Betle gardens, for shade and as a trellis for the support and shelter of the Piper Betle, yields a very pretty pea flower, the red var, seldom used.

Alternanthera sessilis. *Poonanghn Cunney-keeray,* T.— This is a common annual weed in many parts of the country ; greatly prized by the natives, who attribute to it very high qualities, considering the leaves food for Rajahs : it sells at a high price, and the wonder is from such being the case, that the gardeners do not attempt its extensive cultivation, used as greens.

Amaranthus tenuifolius.—*Katoo Sirroo-keeray,* T.—A weed with clusters of green flowers, proceeding from the axils of the leaves, stem much branched ; used similar to the above, found every where.

* Amaranthus spinosus. *Mooloo-keeray*, T.—An annual troublesome weed; abundant; thorny; the small leaves have a dark spot in the centre; it makes tolerable spinach, though troublesome to gather.

* Amaranthus campestris and (polygonoides?) *Sirroo-keeray*, T.—A prevalent weed; commonly cultivated by the native gardeners for spinach—during the hot months, requires to be used when 3 or 4 inches high; of rapid growth; should be sown every third or fourth week.

Amaranthus tristis. *Kuppei-keeray*, T.—Similar to the above.

Amaranthus frumentaceus. *Poongh-keeray*, T.—A large species, cultivated by the Hill people for the seeds, which are ground into flour, and forms one of their principal articles of diet. The leaves are of a reddish brown color, and the plant averages in height from 4 to 6 feet.

* Amaranthus polygamus. *Moollay-keeray*, T.—This vegetable is commonly used during the hot weather. There are three or four varieties, with various colored leaves. It is one of the best of the Indian spinaches; raised from seed during the hot months; and requires to be sown thick and eaten when young. The native gardeners are prone to sow this slily all over the garden, at least on any cultivated spots, the lower class of natives are seldom able to purchase this vegetable, it being too costly; is generally used when 2 feet high under the denomination of Thundoo-keeray, leaves, stems, and roots are eaten at that age.

* Amaranthus oleraceus. *Koollay Thundoo-keeray*, T.— Superior to the above in every respect as a spinach; commonly cultivated in the gardens of Europeans, there are 3 or 4 varieties; one with red leaves, another with white stems, these stems are peeled and eaten as asparagus.

Amaranthus Atropurpureus. *Shegapoo Thundoo-keeray,*
T.—Probably a variety of A. oleraceus, an annual with beautiful red foliage and diminutive flowers, a good spinach seldom
used by Europeans. .

* Amorphophallus campanulatus. *Karroonay-kalungoo,*
T.—The Telinga potatoe. The root of this plant is considered excellent food ; used as potatoes in curries, &c.
The mahogany colored flowers have a most disagreeable
odour ; much cultivated in Madras.

Andropogon esculentum. *Narthum-pilloo,* T.—Used as an
aromatic by some natives to give a scent to water which they
drink. A proportionate quantity imparts a pleasant flavour
to tea.

Aerua lanata. *Kunpoolay-keeray,* T.—A common weed
with woolly silvery looking leaves, and oval heads of white
flowers ; the leaves are used along with others, as mixed
greens, not eaten alone.

* Artocarpus integrifolia. *Pallaw-kai,* T.—The fruit of
the Jack when green used in curries; the outside is cut off
in thin slices and the remainder used ; when ripe, the pulp
and seeds are used for a similar purpose. A few miles
below Coonoor, Neilgherries, these trees produce single fruit,
weighing between 50 and 60lbs.

Asystasia Coromandelina. *Midday-keeray,* T.—A common weed in hedges, flowers either lilac, or white, the leaves
are used mixed with others as greens.

* Atriplex heteranthera. *Thoyah-keeray,* T.—A common
weed ; leaves used as greens, makes an excellent vegetable
to be found in abundance, cultivated.

* Batatas edulis. *Vullee-kalungoo,* T.—The sweet potatoe.
A creeping plant of the Convolvulus tribe ; much cultivated ;

there are two or three varieties; the potatoe like roots are used in various ways, an excellent esculent.

* Bauhinia albida. *Vellay-munthary-poo*, T.—The flower buds of this pretty tree yield an excellent vegetable for curries, not generally known that it can be so used; the flowers are very handsome when open being almost pure white, with a sweet odour.

* Bauhinia purpurea. *Shegaypoo-muntharay-poo*, T.— Similar in quality to the above; the flowers are of a reddish purple color.

* Bergera Kœnigü. *Kurovah-pillay*, T.—A small tree belonging to the Orange tribe; leaves used to flavour curries, mullagatawny, chatnies, &c. and mixed in curry pastes and powders; prepared in this country for transmission to England, and other parts of the world; the mixture of these leaves not only imparts a peculiar flavour to the above, but adds a zest to them. Indigenous, of easy culture.

Boerhavia procumbens. *Mookoorootay-keeray*, T.—A procumbent weed, with small red flowers, used by the natives with other leaves as greens.

Bryonia coccinia. *Covay-kai*, T.—The fruit when green is used in making chatney; common everywhere in hedges and gardens; a troublesome weed.

Byttneria herbacea. *Aree-keeray*, T.—A very common little herbaceous plant with red and yellow flowers, used mixed with others, as greens.

* Caladium esculentum, *Saimmay-keeray*, T.—A species of Arum cultivated for its arrow shaped leaves, which are used as greens both in the East and West Indies; called by the French *Chou de Bresie*, and by the Germans *Essbare. Arum.* The roots are sometimes eaten though not considered wholesome.

Capsella bursa pastoris. *Mullay muntha-keeray,* T.—The shepherds purse, an English weed, common on the Neilgherries, used by the natives as a pot herb.

* Capsicum frutescens. *Moolaykai, Chilley,* T.—Extensively used in curries, &c. There are numerous varieties of chillies in India, many of which are introduced raised from seeds, that have been kept for one year; if any fresher the crop is generally a failure; one species called " devils pepper" introduced by Lord Harris, from Trinidad, is so intensely hot that the natives can hardly manage to use it, cultivated during the cold months.

* Capsicum minimum. *Oosee-moolakyai,* T.—The East Indian bird pepper. Generally cultivated for pickles; they are very hot; this plant is of a shrubby nature, yielding fruit for a series of years. The Caffree Chilley, *Capsicum Grossum* of Botanists. The Nepaul Chilley. *C. Nepalense* are surely not more than varieties of C. frutescens.

Capparis brevispina. *Authoonday-kai,* T.—The green fruit used in making pickles. A scrambling shrub, common in hedges with a beautiful red fruit, the size of a small pear; the stem armed with yellow thorns in pairs at the leaves.

Caralluma adscendens. *Kullee-moolayan,* T.—This curious looking fleshy plant with angular stems belonging to the natural order Asclepiadæ, is used by the natives in making pickles, and sometimes in chatney.

* Carica papaya. *Puppiley-kai,* T.—Used green by Mussulmen, and the lower class of natives as a vegetable. The fruit when ripe used as a dessert.

Cleome pentaphylla, syn. Gynandropsis. *Valay-keeray,* T.—A common weed in cultivated places; A variety with rose colored flowers, is cultivated in flower gardens. The leaves of the wild varieties are used as greens in soups, &c.

Cocos nucifera. *Thennen-coorthoo*, T.—The heart of the cocoapalm; yields an excellent vegetable used similar to Kbnole Kole, it also makes good pickles.

Commelina communis. *Kannang-keeray*, T.—A weed with pretty blue flowers, commonly found in lawns; the leaves are used by the natives; mixed with other greens.

* Coriandrum sativum. *Koothaymully*, T.—The leaves of this annual herb are used by the natives for chatnies. The seeds in decoctions, sweetmeats, &c. Generally cultivated in Madras.

* Cucurbita maxima. *Poosheeny-kai and keeray*, T.— The squash gourd; fruit roundish, generally cultivated, the leaves make excellent greens, and the fruit is used for various culinary purposes; require good soil and abundance of water.

* Cucurbita citrullus, *Pitcha-kai*, T.—The water melon; cultivated in river beds, and in alluvial deposits of lakes, tanks, &c., where abundance of water can be had; used as a dessert.

* Cucurbita ovifera. *Sheemay-poosheeny-kai*, T.—Vegetable marrow. Probably introduced, said to be indigenous at Astrachan; an excellent vegetable; of easy culture in good rich soil. One of the most wholesome of the cucumber tribe.

* Cucumis usitata. *Vellaree-kai*, T.—Cucumber. Commonly cultivated by the natives and eaten when ripe as a dessert. Cucumis sativus and ūtillissimus are also cultivated to a great extent and generally eaten green, without any preparation whatever: the country cucumber is very bitter at both ends, these should be cut off before preparing for salad, probably the above are only varieties of each other.

* Cyamopsis Psoraloides. *Coothah Varay-kai*, T.—An erect annual; cultivated during the cold months in gardens for the little flat pods, which are used in curries, and as

French beans, grows from 2 to 3 feet high ; the pods are seldom very tender.

Cynodon dactylon. *Hurrum-pilloo*, T.—Hurryalee-grass. —The young and tender leaves of this grass are used in chatnies, a rather curious use, but considered very pleasant, the roots make a cooling drink.

Dillenia speciosa. *Ovay-kai*, T.—The fruit of this large and handsome tree is used by the lower class of natives in their curries, having an agreeable acid flavour; and also in chatnies.

Desmanthus natans. *Soonday-keeray*, T.—The floating sensitive plant; generally found floating in tanks; the leaflets are used by the natives, though not generally.

* Dioscorea purpurea. *Poothooschary vulle Kelangoo*, T.—Pondicherry sweet potatoe. Not much used in Madras. A yam, the roots are boiled and eaten as a potatoe.

* Dioscorea Aculeata. *Kantoo Kelangoo*, T.—The Goa potatoe. I am not aware if this yam is much cultivated in Madras. There are many species of the yam cultivated for various purposes, Dioscorea triphylla is used to render the Cocoanut tree toddy more intoxicating. D. Pentaphylla, the flowers are used as greens, and the tubers as an esculent. D. bulbifera for a similar purpose. The Genus is very extensive ; some of the species are said to be poisonous. All creepers.

* Dolichos ensiformis. *Thumbatun-koy*, T.—A species of bean which climbs to a great distance. The pods are used as a substitute for French beans; before cooking, they are cut into thin slices, commonly cultivated ; require very strong stakes.

D. uniflorus and D. Sinensis are cultivated for the same purpose.

Erythroxylon areolatum. *Davaahdarum-keeray*, T.—The

tender leaves of this tree are used as greens mostly by the jungle people ; the flowers are very small of a yellowish green color.

Euphorbia pilulifera. *Umaum patcheh-arise*, T.—An abundant weed to be found every where ; used but seldom, mixed with others as greens.

Ficus racemosus. *Attai kai*, T.—The fruit of this large tree is used in various ways, dried, in curries, roasted and eaten, pickles are likewise made with them ; common every where.

* Fœniculum Vulgare. *Shohie-keeray*, T.—Fennel, used as seasoning by the natives, and by Europeans in garnishing ; common in gardens, raised from seed.

Gisekia Pharnaceoides. *Munnelle-keeray*, T.—The leaves of this weed are used by the natives in the preparation of dholl.

Glinus trianthemoides. *Sharunnay-keeray*, T.—A procumbent herb with fleshy leaves of a brownish color ; used as spinach ; a very abundant and troublesome weed.

* Hibiscus Sabdariffa. *Sheemay kashlee-keeray*, T.—The Roselle. The leaves are used as greens, alone, and mixed with others. The calyx and capsules when freed of seeds are made into Jellies, and Tarts; generally cultivated ; the flowers of this plant are very pretty, often cultivated in flower beds.

Hibiscus surattensis. *Kashlee-keeray*, T.—A herbaceous plant with speckled prickly stems and yellow flowers; the leaves are used as greens, indigenous. H. Cannabinus, the leaves of which are a little sour, used as the above.

Hoya Viridiflora. *Cooringee-keeray*, T.—A climbing

shrub with umbels of green flowers; the leaves are used by the natives in small quantities, mixed with others.

Ipomœa sepiaria. *Thalee-keeray*, S.—A climbing perennial plant of the convolvulous tribe with rose colored flowers, found in hedges; the leaves are eaten mixed with others as greens.

Ipomœa reptans. *Vellay-keeray*, T.—A creeping annual of the convolvulous family with rose colored flowers, found about the borders of tanks and moist places. The leaves are used as greens.

Ipomœa reniformis. *Perrettay-keeray*, T.—A perennial creeper with yellow flowers; the leaves used as greens mixed with tamarind; very common during the cold months.

* Lablab Vulgaris. *Avaray-kai*, T.—The pods of this plant are used as a substitute for French beans, the beans in curries; commonly cultivated in gardens, of easy growth, a pandal is required for its support.

* Lagenaria Vulgaris. *Soriaie-kai*, T.—Bottle gourd. Commonly cultivated by the natives to whom it is of some importance as food; of easy culture, seldom eaten by Europeans, it being very coarse.

* Lagenaria pipo. *Pooshnec-kai*, T.—The Pumpkin. Similar to the above, much used by the natives.

Leucas Aspera, Syn : Phlomis esculentum. *Thoombay-keeray*, T.—A small annual weed with white flowers; appears during the rains; the leaves are used as greens mixed with others.

* Mangifera Indica. *Mangoy*, T.—The green fruit of the Mango used in making chatnies, pickles and curries.

In the Bombay Territories, the mangoes when full grown
are cut into slices, dried in the sun and preserved, they
form an article of commerce; used in acidulating curries,
mullagatawnies, &c.

* Momordica Charantia Var. muricata. *Pavay-kai.*
T.—The bitter gourd. Commonly cultivated and used in
curries, said to be very wholesome; another fruit called
Nerree pavay-kai, is sold in the bazaars, I have seen nothing but the fruit, and take it to belong to Cucurbitaceæ.

* Momordica charantia. *Punney Podaylang-kai*, T.—The
green fruit used in curries, &c., it grows about 1 foot or 15
inches in length, commonly cultivated, known by the name of
small snake gourd; before cooking it is generally steeped in
salt water.

Morinda umbellata. *Noona-kai*, T.—The fruit of this
tree when green, used as pickles.

* Moringa Pterogospermum. *Mooroongay-kai-keeray and
poo*, T.—This is a very useful tree. The leaves and flowers
are much eaten by the natives, and make an excellent
vegetable. The pods are freely eaten by Europeans as
asparagus, either boiled separately or in curries—the roots
as a substitute for horse radish—the natives have recourse
to this root in adulterating the country mustard, prepared
here for sale, and very often pass it off for genuine English;
cultivated every where, in gardens and about villages. The
large branches planted in the ground root freely and soon
become small trees, giving a continued supply of wholesome
vegetables; produce from seedling plants is the best.

* Musa Sapientum. *Vallee-kai*, T.—The common plantain. The green fruit used in curries; the natives use the

extremities of the flower shoots, the heart of the stem, and that portion of it from which the roots proceed in their curries.

Nelumbium speciosum. *Thamaray-kalungoo*, T.—The roots of the sacred bean of India after being cut into slices, dried and fried in oil, are eaten by the natives and considered a delicacy.

* Ocymum Villosum. *Tolashee*, T.—An aromatic herb, leaves used for seasonings, of easy cultivation. In all Courts of Justice, the Hindoos are sworn by these leaves, which are placed on the palm of the hand by a Brahmin, who repeats the prescribed oath, and at the termination, they are masticated and swallowed. A good number of this genera are used in cookery.

* Oxalis corniculatus. *Pooliaray-keeray*, T.—A common weed on lawns and in gardens—used by the natives in making chatney; and in curries, a good substitute for lime juice or tamarind imparting a peculiar acid taste.

* Phyllanthus embilica. Syn, Embilca Officinalis, *Toap-poo Nelley-kai*, T.—The fruit of this tree is used in making pickles and preserves; generally cultivated in native gardens.

* Pisonia morindifolia. *Lutchee-kottay-ellay*, T.—The Lettuce tree. The leaves of this pretty tree are used in various ways; sometimes by Europeans; they make tolerable greens cooked with cocoanut, chillies, &c., &c., to be found only in gardens, leaves of a light green color, turning nearly white during the hot months.

* Portulacca oleracea. *Piropoo-keeray*, T.—A common weed; cultivated by the market gardeners; used as spinach and in curries; almost tasteless.

* Portulacca quadrifida. *Passeeray-keeray*, T.—A small

troublesome weed with fleshy leaves used as greens, common every where.

Premna integrifolia. *Passoo-munnæ-keeray*, T.—The leaves of this tree have a very unpleasant odour when pressed in the hand ; used by the natives in soups and curry.

Premna serratifolia. *Munnæ-keeray*, T.—Leaves used similar to those of the above. The natives are very fond of these two species.

* Psophocarpus tetragonolobus. Goa Beans.—A bean commonly cultivated and used as French beans ; easily known by its having 4 fringed membraneous edges, much used by Europeans, called by the French *Chevaux-de Frase*. The plant is indigenous in the Mauritius.

Rivea fragrans. *Boodthee-keeray*, T.—A beautiful variety of the convolvulous tribe ; flowers transparent white, opening at sunset and perfuming the air with a very pleasant odour ; leaves used as greens, found in hedges, called the clove scented creeper by Europeans.

Rothia trifoliata. *Nurrey-pithen-keeray*, T.—A small procumbent weed, with trifoliate leaves, used by the natives as greens, abundant every where.

* Rumex vesicaria. *Sookkhagn-keeray*, T.—Sorrel. Cultivated for greens, &c., grows plentifully about Madras in the fields during the rains.

* Salsola Indica. *Oomarie-keeray*, T.—A small procumbent weed, with linear shaped leaves having no stalks, found in salt marshes ; the leaves used as greens, a very pleasant vegetable.

Solanum incertum. *Mannuttha-Kalee*, T.—The leaves are

used as a pot herb. The fruit and leaves in the preparation of chatnies ; cultivated by the natives commonly.

* Solanum Melongena. *Kutheerce-kai,* T.—The Brinjal : or Egg-plant. One of the most useful of Indian vegetables ; used in culinary purposes in various ways. The large Cape varieties are the best ; commonly cultivated and used by Europeans and Natives ; require good soil and abundance of water.

* Solanum Lycopersicum. *Thuck-kalee.*—The Tomato. *Love apple or wolf peach* ; cultivated in gardens for the fruit which is used for sauces, chatnies, garnishing, soups, &c. ; produces the best fruit when trained on a trellis, more a luxury than valuable as a vegetable.

Solanum torvum. *Soonday-kai,* T.—Used as a vegetable by the natives, a weed.

Sonchus oleraceus. *Kaat-moolingee-keeray,* T.—The Sow Thistle ; used in the Neilgherries as a pot herb by the natives.

* Spinacea oleracea and New Zealand Spinach. *Vusay-ley-keeray,* T.—Spinach, commonly cultivated in all gardens.

Spondias Mangifera. *Mirreymangi-kai,* T.—The Hog plum. The leaves of this tree are used in the preparation of chatnies. The green fruit used as pickles.

Stellaria media. *Kaaray-Muntha-keeray,* T.—Chickweed. This English weed is used by the natives on the Neilgherries as a pot herb, eaten alone, and mixed with others, probably introduced.

Sureda Indica. *Koyey-Passceray-keeray,* T.—A procumbent weed with pea green leaves, found in salt marshes, sometimes in gardens, used in native culinary as spinach.

* Tamarindus Indicus. *Pollium-Cooloondoo and kai.* T.—

The young leaves used in pepper water ; the green fruit as an ingredient in chatnies, and the pulp of the ripe fruit in curries.

Trianthema obcordata. *Sharvalay-keeray*, T.—A troublesome weed, springs up every where ; the young leaves used as spinach, when somewhat old mixed with others and used as greens.

Tribulus terrestris. *Nerringee-keeray*, T.—A procumbent annual weed with thorny capsules, yellow flowers, leaflets are eaten mixed along with others ; seldom used but in time of scarcity.

* Trichosanthes anguiua. *Poodalungai*, T.—The snake gourd. Generally cultivated for its long snake-like fruit used in curries, often used cut into lengths filled with a preparation of minced meat, much liked by East Indians.

Trigonella Fœnum Græcum. *Vendee-keeray*, T.—Commonly cultivated for a pot herb, considered very wholesome, imparts a very strong odour and taste to curries, the seeds are said to be slightly tonic.

Vitis Quadrangularis. *Perrunday*, T.—This trailing, and creeping plant with 4 angled and winged stems is used by the Natives as greens, and in the preparation of chatney ; cultivated about villages.

Webera tetrendra. *Carray-keeray*, T.—The leaves of this thorny shrub are eaten as greens, common about Madras ; produces a small fruit about the size of a pea which the Natives eat.

* Zizyphus Jujuba. *Yellenden-kai*, T.—The wild Bere fruit, used in chatnies and pickles, a very common tree in Madras. The Natives are very fond of the fruit when nearly ripe, it tastes like a Crab Apple.

INDIAN VEGETABLES.

Abelmoschus esculentus
Achryanthes aspera
Æschynomene aspera
Agati grandiflora
Alternanthera sessilis
Amaranthus tenuifolius
„ spinosus
„ campestris
„ tristis
„ frumentaceus
„ polygamus
„ oleraceus
„ atropurpureus
Amorpophalus campanulatus
Andropogon esculentum
Acrua lanata
Artocarpus integrifolius
Asystasia Coromandeliana
Atriplex heteranthera
Batatas edulis.
Bauhinia albida
„ purpurea
Bergera Kœnigii
Boerhavia procumbens
Bryonia coccinia
Byttneria herbacea
Caladium esculentum
Capsella bursa-pastoris
Capsicum frutescens
„ minimum
Capparis brevispina

Caralluma adscendens
Carica papaya
Cleome pentaphylla
Cocos nucifera
Commelina communis
Coriandrum sativum
Cucurbita maxima
„ citrullus
„ ovifera
Cucumus usitata
Cyamopsis psoraloides
Cynodon dactylon
Dillenia speciosa
Desmanthus natans
Dioscorea purpurea
„ aculeata
Dolichos ensiformis
Erythroxylon areolatum
Euphorbia pilulifera
Emblica Officinalis
Ficus racemosus
Foeniculum vulgare
Gisekia pharnaceoides
Glinus trianthemoides
Hibiscus sabdariffa
„ surattensis
Hoya viridiflora

Ipomœa separia
„ reptans
„ reniformis

Lablab vulgaris

Lagenaria vulgaris

" pipo

Leptadenia reticulata

Leucas aspera

Mangifera Indica

Momordica charantia var. muricata

Momordica charantia

Morinda umbellata

Moringa pterogospermum

Musa sapientum

Nelumbium speciosum

Ocymum villosum

Oxalis corniculatus

Pisonia morindifolia

Portulacca oleracea

Portulacca quadrifida

Premna integrifolia

" serratifolia

Psophocarpus tetragonolobus

Rivea fragrans

Rothia trifoliata

Rumex vesicaria

Salsola Indica

Solanum incertum

" melongena

" Lycopersicum

" torvum

Sonchus oleraceus

Spinacia oleracea

Spondias mangifera

Stellaria media

Suœda Indica

Tamarindus Indica

Trianthema obcordata

Tribulus terrestris

Trichosanthes anguina

Vitis quadrangularis

Webera tetrandra

Zizyphus jujuba

PREFACE.

It is with feelings of pride mingled with satisfaction, that reference can be made to the success of the former issues of this series of "*Brochures*," their circulation is probably unprecedented in the Gardening Literature of Southern India, above 2,500 copies have been circulated, simplicity of detail has invariably been attended to, technicalities in a language belonging to a race "long since swept from the face of the earth" have been avoided, the object of the writer being the imparting of instruction in a style that would meet the wants of all, to advance the *Art of Horticulture* in our "plain mother tongue," thereby avoiding obscurity in imparting that which is intended for instruction. As promised in the last issue, the importance of vegetable culture in India was to be resumed in No. 5, in order to fulfil this end the present No. makes its appearance as a Calendar of operations for the Kitchen and Flower garden, adapted to Madras, as the rain commences at different periods in the various districts, residents in which will find but little difficulty in adapting the following Calendar to their wants, by commencing their operations, with the setting in of the annual rains, or dividing the months into seasons suitable to the district, as shown at page 20, No. 2. In returning thanks to the public for their extensive patronage, the writer holds out no promise of these Pamphlets being continued, however unforeseen circumstances may induce him to do so, ? ?

OPERATIONS IN THE KITCHEN GARDEN.

JANUARY.

As the weather during the month will generally be clear and dry, attention to watering is required, if possible water in the morning otherwise late in the evening, never water vegetables during the heat of the day. The sowing of European vegetables may now be discontinued, as in the majority of cases seed sown during this month will prove to be labor needlessly expended, they will not come to maturity, or scarcely to a state fit for consumption. Last month may be considered as drawing to a close all successful operations in regard to European vegetable sowing, with the exception of a few salads, which may be sown in beds, shaded and hand-watered, with attention they will produce small crops. During the first and second week is a good time to sow cucumbers, vegetable marrow, gourds and such like. Nepaul spinach should be sown and planted for a supply during the hot months. Attend to keeping the soil hoed amongst growing crops, eradicating weeds to prevent their seeding, which they now do freely, continue to earth up celery, choosing a dry day for directions as to *earthing.* See No. 3, page 38. Plant cuttings of the cabbage tribe in beds if rooted they will give a good supply of sprouts during the hot months. Sow country vegetables if required, remove all decaying vegetables to the compost heap. Look to the graft mangoes, continue every two or three days to deepen the incision till the branch is cut through. If any are entirely removed they may be planted without delay, taking care to support them against damage from high winds.

FLOWER GARDEN.

The flowers during this month should be in great perfection. The main operations consist in keeping everything clean and in perfect order, using the knife amongst shrubs, &c., where required. Attend to the young shoots of creepers so that they may be properly trained, cut back all plants that may be growing over the edges of the beds or walks, this should be done neatly so that the use of the knife may not be discovered, nothing looks worse than plants abruptly cut round the hedge of flower beds. Such cuttings of shrubs, and roses, as are rooted should be planted out in beds, well watered, and shaded for a few days. Attend to plants in pots, roses in flower-bud will be improved by frequent watering with liquid manure, it will increase the size of the flowers. Shade tender plants from the midday sun, keep a supply of water exposed to the sun during the day, for watering potted plants in the evening. Attend to clipping hedges, keeping the walks and grass in proper trim.

Remarks.—The weather during the month is generally clear, rain seldom falls, dews are plentiful, vegetables are abundant towards the end of the month. Fruit, such as oranges, pomegranates, guavas, plantains, &c., are to be had.

FEBRUARY.

KITCHEN GARDEN.

As the Horticulture Exhibition is generally held during the early part of the month, attend to the schedule of prizes if you intend to compete, preserve such articles as may be required by marking them with stakes; in forwarding articles for competition pay marked attention to what is required, avoid sending vegetables of any kind in flower pots. In the garden little is required beyond the directions of last month, a few salads may be sown, country radishes, cucumbers and gourds may still be sown. Keep the garden clear from decayed leaves, vegetables during this month, especially the cabbage tribe give out a most disagreeable odour if left decaying. See that arrangements are made to keep up a supply of such country vegetables as may be required. Watering will invariably be requisite throughout the month, plant out (if on hand) cuttings of the cabbage tribe. Attend to collecting manure for next season.

FLOWER GARDEN.

The directions of last month are suitable to this, little more can be done than attending to watering, and cleanliness, let plants in pots intended for exhibition be protected from the midday sun if possible. During the course of the month, remove and put in pots a good supply of verbenas and such like, to preserve them during the hot season. Attend to plants in pots, frequently stirring up the soil on the surface. If worms are troublesome, a little clear lime water used occasionally will remove them.

Remarks.—The weather during the month is clear and calm, dew every morning, rain seldom occurs if ever; vegetables and flowers, in most seasons are plentiful; fruit, such as sapodilas, mangoes, oranges, custard apples, &c., are to be had.

MARCH.
KITCHEN GARDEN.

As the cultivation of European vegetables will no longer give any degree of satisfaction equivalent to the expense incurred; it is not necessary to presume that by giving directions, success will be the reward of carrying them out. The heat is too great to develop seeds of northern climes, indeed it is mere chance to succeed in germinating and growing tropical seeds. Attention to the culture of such varieties of country vegetables as may be required is all that is requisite in cultivation, though the latter may be purchased in the market much cheaper than they can be grown in private gardens. All vacant spaces in the garden should now be dug, and thrown up in ridges (this is applicable to heavy soils) so as to expose the soil to influence of the sun during the hot weather. Where the soil is light let it be dug over level, collect manure without delay, if composed of heating materials it will require to be watered and turned over frequently, be sure this matter is not over-looked, attend to watering lately planted Mango trees, untying the ligatures round the grafted parts, support the stems securely against high winds, store Yams in sand or dry soil.

FLOWER GARDEN.

Little can be done during this month, pay attention to clean-liness, watering shrubs, roses, &c., such beds as are empty should be neatly dug over; look to the roots of Dahlias, let them be stored in pots of sand, or the pots they were grown in if the soil is dried *they must be kept dry*, gloxinias, achimenes, and bulbs, require the same treatment, plants growing in pots should be placed if possible to receive the morning sun and shaded during midday.

Remarks.—The weather during this month is clear, hot, and very unpleasant, from the prevailing southerly winds, slight dew frequently. No rain falls during the whole course of the month; European vegetables are very scarce, dear, and bad in general; country vegetables plentiful, such as brinjals, radishes, greens, &c. Fruit none, with the exception of indifferent plantains.

APRIL.

KITCHEN GARDEN.

This month might be passed over in silence, as little or nothing can be done unless digging up any portions of the garden not attended to last month, this should not be neglect-ed any longer. Cucumbers, gourds and melons may be sown during the month, they require protection from the sun until established. Attend to fruiting pines, if the crowns appear to grow too large let the hearts be taken out neatly, remove all suckers from the bottom of the fruit, after the fruit has swelled a good size, water should be sparingly applied as it tends to injure the flavour.

FLOWER GARDEN.

The directions of last month are suitable to this, little more can be done than keeping the garden clean and free of weeds, towards the end of the month look well to the support of young trees, creepers, &c., as gales may be expected early in May. Prepare soil for plants in pots without delay : directions for compost, see No. 3 ; look over dahlia roots, &c., in case they are being injured by vermin. Roses in pots should not be excited at present, or they will be weakened.

Remarks.—The weather during the month is similar to that of last, wind changeable from S. to E. and W., dew is seldom seen. A few slight showers of rain sometimes occur ; European vegetables are very scarce, native vegetables plentiful. Fruit, such as grapes, pine-apples, and some of the orange tribe are to be had. Plantains are plentiful.

MAY.

KITCHEN GARDEN.

During the month the land wind commences, much difficulty will be experienced in cultivating any but the common varieties of country vegetables, dig over any vacant spaces of ground no matter how roughly ; prepare manure ; repair and build water channels when required ; make and repair roads and walks.

FLOWER GARDEN.

Now is a good time to put walks in good order and make others where required. If composts for seeds and plants in pots are not preparing, delay no longer, as they will be required in July. Wash all empty flower pots and order supplies of new ones, use every endeavour to put down the unsightly pots in general use—it can be done.

Remarks.—The weather during the month is unpleasantly hot from the prevailing land winds, in most seasons a few slight showers of rain fall, seldom other than country vegetables are to be had, with the exception of cabbage sprouts, which are hard and tough ; mangoes and pine-apples are plentiful and cheap ; flowers are scarce.

JUNE.

KITCHEN GARDEN.

Although rain frequently occurs during the month, it is scarcely desirable to recommend the sowing of European vegetables. It is more requisite to push forward any new work that may be required, dig over and trench all vacant and new ground that may be taken in for cultivation. Be careful that a good supply of manure is on hand.

FLOWER GARDEN.

Preparing pits for planting trees and ornamental shrubs may be proceeded with, likewise the filling up of all hollows on the lawns where water accumulates during monsoon. Making new flower gardens where required, they should be proceeded with at once, it will save time when the gardeners are required for more active operations in July and August. Repair walks, and make new ones, see that they are broad and level enough for two persons to walk abreast upon them, there is no necessity to raise them up like ridges in the centre, if they are slightly convex to throw off the water, it is sufficient.

Remarks.—The weather during this month is similar to that of last; showers are more frequent; European vegetables are rarely to be had. Fruit is plentiful.

JULY.

KITCHEN GARDEN.

Everything should be prepared during the present month for sowing seeds in August. If the weather is at all favorable, sow a small quantity of celery and parsley for early plants. Peas may be sown towards the latter part of the month, though with but slight chance of success in the generality of seasons, during the last week the levelling of the soil thrown up in ridges may be proceeded with. The manure heap should be in a fit condition for use.

FLOWER GARDEN.

Little can be done during the month further than preparation for the ensuing seed time, let composts be in a perfect state for use before the end of the month. Make up grass edgings with turf. Do not prune roses unless they show signs of growth, this can be easily discovered by the swelling and bursting of the buds, if they show such signs, prune and manure; though waiting till the following month, would be more judicious. Take care not to be carried into too active operations by a good shower of rain. Look to the roots of dahlias, gloxinias and achimenes, they may have commenced to grow, retard them as much as possible, but bring them to the light, as dahlias are very impatient, their roots should be divided towards the end of the month into as many divisions as possible with a sharp knife, having a shoot upon each division.

Remarks.—The rains of the S. W. Monsoon commence during this month in slight showers, the sky is very cloudy : rain is frequent in most seasons. Fruit and vegetables are scarce.

AUGUST.

KITCHEN GARDEN.

As imported seeds should now be on hand, let a first sowing be put in pots or boxes without delay. If the weather is favorable, successive sowings may be put in during the whole course of the month. Care must be taken that the soil is in a proper moist condition as described in No. 1, page 8. Guard against the ravages of red ants; be sparing of water to imported seeds until they germinate. A first sowing of peas and French beans may be put in, likewise carrots, beet, parsley and radishes, choose a dry day, sow celery in boxes or pots in rich soil mixed with well decayed manure, and a small quantity of powdered lime. The reason celery is so apt to run to seed, arises from inattention to keep up a constant luxuriance by the aid of good manure, celery should never receive a check ; of country vegetables, sow brinjals, gourds, cucumbers, roselles, greens, spinach, beans, chillies, snake gourds, &c., plant yams and Jerusalem artichokes. Attend to top-dressing asparagus beds, make a fresh bed of water-cresses in a shady spot near a well or tank where they can be easily supplied with water twice a day. Put in suckers of pine-apples ; prepare stocks of mangoes for grafting. Let the garden soil be levelled, well-manured and dug over ; make sure the manure is well-looked after and mixed with lime and ashes before using.

FLOWER GARDEN.

Sow seeds of everything that can be had most suitable for the climate, be careful how small seeds are sown and watered, read directions in No. 1, look to the roots of dahlias, gloxinias, &c., they should be set a-growing in good soil. If no plan has been definitely fixed upon to secure a good supply of flowers, now is the time to look to it, there is no time to spare ; propagate verbenas by layers, sow holyhocks, phloxes, petunias, balsams, &c., increase your stock of chrysanthemums, by division, or fresh supplies, let the flower garden be well-dug and manured, dig and manure round the roots of shrubs on lawns, &c. Let a shaded piece of ground be prepared in which to put cuttings of roses, shrubs, &c., prepare pits for planting trees and shrubs, make them large and deep. Pits in the soil of Madras or anywhere should not be less than $2\frac{1}{4}$ feet in diameter and depth. Too much care cannot be taken of seedlings, lest they get drawn during the dull days that prevail, expose them to the light and air as much as possible. Top-dress all plants in pots not intended to be repotted with fresh soil and manure, repot and top-dress roses in pots. Prune and manure garden roses and put in cuttings.

Remarks.—It were unnecessary to write these instructions if those for whom they are written do not carry them out during the course of this month. As success can only be looked for by close attention, next month will be of less avail to have plants sufficiently strong to produce an early crop or to stand the heavy rains, and whatever complaints may have to be made anent the failure of vegetables and the display of flowers, in January and February, it can be ascribed to no other cause than neglecting to conduct operations at the right season and in a proper manner. The native gardeners are not so much to blame, as they in general go by the instructions they receive.

Rain is frequent during the month ; country vegetables are plentiful ; fruit and European vegetables are very scarce.

SEPTEMBER.

KITCHEN GARDEN.

This is a proper time to sow a succession of peas, French beans and spinach, they may be put in every week during the month, continue to sow vegetables of all kinds. Onions and Leeks in light rich soil in beds, protected from the rains by mats tied over moveable bamboo framework. Attend to the seedlings sown last month, some of which will be ready for transplanting. Knol-khol and cabbage, if any were sown early in July, will be ready for final transplanting in the garden, in beds or rows, let them be lifted carefully, disturb the roots as little as possible. Encourage the growth of celery by slight waterings of liquid manure, look after insects, a slight sprinkling of lime over and under the leaves will arrest their ravages, if not used let them be picked off with the hand every morning. Lime will in no wise injure the tenderest vegetation if slaked and cool. Native vegetables sown at the beginning of last month will be fit for planting out. Commence to graft mangoes, make preparations such as digging trenches, &c., to prevent the garden being flooded during the monsoon near at hand. Manure pine apples, remove the suckers and put them into root.

FLOWER GARDEN.

Petunias, holyhocks, phloxes, &c., &c., sown last month should during this be fit for planting out, choosing a dull damp day.

Continue to sow balsams, holyhocks, and all showy annuals, not neglecting mignonette. Balsam seed from Hyderabad is generally good, and from the cultivators there removing the lateral branches, they have acquired a peculiar upright habit, show about one foot of blossom in a column when well-grown. Attend to cleanliness and keeping the soil in flower bed open by hoeing (*the idea of seeing a Gardener sitting in a flower bed digging it up with a piece of bamboo is absurd.*) Prune roses if hitherto neglected, layer bud and put in cuttings of roses and such shrubs, trees and creepers as may be required. Sow seeds of trees and shrubs, where layering is required, attend to the instructions given in No. 2, page 16, put in pipings of carnations, picotees in boxes, filled with fine sand mixed with red earth. Let all creepers be neatly tied to the posts or trellises upon which they are trained, prune where required, prune and keep in proper form shrubs, &c., attend to cutting hedges and filling up gaps, casuarina hedges neatly trimmed would be much neater round flower gardens than unsightly bamboo trellises, it is astonishing they are not more generally planted, as they combine neatness with economy, are easily raised if the seed is not too deeply covered with soil.

OCTOBER.

KITCHEN GARDEN.

Transplant all vegetable plants, large enough into beds or drills where they are to grow. Trenches should be ready to receive celery plants, shade if the weather is clear, look after tomatoes, onions, leeks, carrots and beet-root, let them be thinned out to proper distances from each other, the thinnings may be planted if required. Continue to sow a few varieties of vegetable seeds. Peas may be sown every week, let the drills in which they are sown be raised above the surface level : continue to sow a succession of French beans. Keep up a supply of salads, such as lettuce, endive, mustard, water-cress, &c. Finish early in the month preparations for planting out vegetables, do not trust till wanted as the soil may not be workable from rain. Let everything about the garden be neat and clean, eradicate weeds on their first appearance. If the weather during the month should prove dry, peas and the cabbage tribe will suffer much. A supply of water will be requisite to prevent the crops sustaining a check which would prove very detrimental. When water is applied let it be in the morning, very early, if possible, when it is cool, frequent hoeing up the soil amongst the crops will require to be looked too. If activity is not displayed during the early part of this month in forwarding operations, there is but little chance of success for the season. Take particular care the crops are not planted on the same piece of ground they were last year ; alternate them yearly if possible. Graft mangoes, and plant pine-apples.

FLOWER GARDEN.

The operations of last month are applicable to this. Look after dahlias in pots, stake them and water occasionally with liquid manure. Plant out verbenas, heliotropes and all other bedding plants. Keep up a supply of balsams, cockscombs, mignonette, &c. Plant trees and shrubs, attend to training and pruning creepers. This is a good time to get roses, fuschias, violets, &c., from the Hills of Bangalore. Take advantage of dry days to cut grass, straighten and trim the edges of walks and beds. Give everything a neat and clean appearance. Protect all newly planted trees from wind. The best plan is, use three-tarred ropes for each plant, fix them to the stems, round which should be tied a piece of canvass to prevent the friction of the ropes from injuring the bark, tie the ropes tight to three pegs firmly driven into the ground at the proper distance from the plants. This is costlier than stakes but more permanent, and will protect the plants till properly rooted.

Remarks.—The weather during the month is generally wet, and stormy, more especially during the latter part of it. Vegetables and fruits still continue scarce.

NOVEMBER.

KITCHEN GARDEN.

Few European vegetables will come to perfection if not fit to plant out during this month. Attend to transplanting seedlings, peas and French beans may be sown every week or ten days, the main crop must be looked for from seed sown this month as peas sown in December seldom succeed. Sow a small quantity of cabbage, knol-khol, cauliflower, tomatoes, &c., likewise a few salads. Cauliflower sown during the first week of the month if they are well attended to, flowers may be had during February. Attend to transplanting onions and leeks. Thin out turnips and carrots to proper distances from each other. Plant celery in trenches, look after all details, such as cleanliness, digging trenches to carry off the heavy rains, put in cuttings of cabbage sprouts for use during the hot season. Graft mangoes, put in cuttings of figs and vines. Plant onion bulbs for salad.

FLOWER GARDEN.

Continue to transplant seedlings into pots or boxes. Plant out annuals, verbenas, holyhocks, phloxes and ipomeas, if strong enough. Sow any flower seeds remaining on hand. Sow seeds of trees and shrubs. Prepare early in the month stations for ornamental creepers, and plant without delay. Attend to training creepers and pruning where required. Prune and manure garden roses and put in cuttings. In pruning, cut the old branches down to three or four eyes from the bottom. Topdress all plants in pot not requiring re-potting, protect tender plants from heavy rains, activity is required during this month to obtain a good supply of flowers during the three following months. The finer varieties of roses in pots should be re-potted if necessary, they require a heavy soil mixed with well-decayed cowdung. Support all plants requiring it from the high winds.

Remarks.—The weather during the month is in general boisterous, with heavy rains, the N. E. Monsoon continues with great violence. Vegetables and flowers continue scarce.

DECEMBER.

KITCHEN GARDEN.

Continue to plant out and transplant into boxes all vegetable plants on hand during the first week. Attend to thinning turnips and carrots. Plant celery in trenches and earth up such as may require it. Keep the soil amongst the growing crops hoed, and eradicate weeds on their first appearance. Blanch lettuce and endive by tying up the leaves. Thin out the branches of tomatoes. Look sharp after insects amongst cabbage and cauliflower. Use slaked lime freely on all crops attacked : it will prove a beneficial check. During the month sow cucumbers, vegetable marrow, country vegetables for greens, &c. Early planted vegetables will bo fit for use towards the end of the month. French beans and salads should be in abundance. Attend to staking peas, beans, &c. Continue to make up a manure heap for the ensuing season ; let nothing be lost in the shape of vegetable matter. The main work of the month is attention to growing crops ; look to early grafted mangoes ; make incisions gradually on the branches above the grafts.

FLOWER GARDEN.

Plant out the remaining stock of annuals ; sow a few holy-hocks, amaranthus, &c. A last sowing of balsams may be put in. Sow convolvoluses of all kinds. Petunias for flowering during the hot months. Attend to dahlias and encourage them by frequent watering of liquid manure. Keep the flower beds and walks clean and neat ; water and roll the walks towards the latter part of the month, it will give them a neat appearance, at the same time they will be more comfortable to walk upon.

Remarks.—The weather during the first two weeks is similar to last month, generally clearing up towards the latter end. Fogs are frequent ; flowers still continue scarce with the exception of roses ; vegetables are scarce ; country greens, &c., are to be had in abundance ; fruit, such as oranges, guavas and plantains are plentiful.

IMPROVEMENT OF NATIVE GARDENERS.

" *Ed. io anche sono pittore.*"—" And I also will be a painter."
" Such was the exclamation of a peasant as he surveyed one
of Raphael's sublime productions," no doubt his imagination
led him to consider that all requisites necessary to be a painter
consisted in the possession of a few brushes, pencils and a yard
or two of Canvas. Were matters rightly viewed, it would
readily be discovered that the peasant mentioned above, is not
a character of rare occurrence, dupes of imagination are very
frequent with reference to gardening in India. The knowledge
of gardening is pre-eminently a work of time, and the wonder
is that its progress in Southern India is not of a more satisfactory nature, seeing so many have tried it. That a reason must
exist for such a standstill state of matters as the *Art of Gardening* still presents is evident. And that it exists in the ignorance of the Native gardeners is but too plain to be denied. It
is scarcely possible that Horticulture can be permitted to stand
aloof from further progress ; it being an Art, the furtherance of
which tends to contribute so much towards producing a supply of
wholesome food for human consumption. In Tropical countries
above all others the cultivation of vegetables cannot be fostered
with too much care, considering their value as an article of diet.
The object aimed at in these remarks is not to expose the
ignorance of the Native gardeners, but rather to give publicity
to an idea, the object of which is the removal of the draw-
backs that exist to the furtherance of Horticulture. It is evident
the Native gardeners cannot be sent to increase their knowledge
of Horticulture amongst the " musty cobwebs of college lore."
Schools of Arts and such like are in operation, and why should
there not be a school of Horticulture conducted by a practical
Master. The expense would be comparatively trifling. A few
acres of land conveniently situated for a good supply of water—
where all the operations of a regular kitchen garden could be
carried out. 18 or 20 youths *apprenticed* could be taught every

thing that is requisite to make them good and efficient in two
or three years. The value realized from the produce, &c., would
undoubtedly be sufficient to pay for the support of the establish-
ment, with exception of the Master's salary which might be dis-
bursed by Government. There are Horticulture Societies it is
true, but any one who has paid attention to these institutions
will find that in the generality of cases through the lapse of time,
they direct their efforts away from the objects for which they
were instituted. The idea of an institution for teaching gardening alone may be new in India, though it is the only plan that
appears feasible, and by which a real knowledge of gardening
can be imparted. It may cause a smile, *nay* it may even be
laughed at, still it is not an uncommon thing to see the
paradox of yesterday the truism of to-day, Steamers traverse
round the Globe, Towns are lighted with gas, but who does
not know that Lardner laughed at the one, and Davy at the
other; there is not a doubt but that with fair attention and
well directed skill, vegetables may be produced in Madras to
please the most fastidious, but not until such time as the
primitive *modus operandi* and the patriarchal prejudices of
the natives are removed. If instruction is to be imparted it
must be done thoroughly or not at all ; and it will invariably
be appropriated by the native if his eye can be fixed steadily
upon the equivalent, for his gaining it, viz., Rupees, Annas
and Pice. If that is not the goal which can be reached, few
will seek instruction for the love of it.

The question may be asked how much instruction would
you impart to the Native gardener? It cannot be answered
better than by quoting an able writer on education ; "As much
as he can possibly attain—the more the better for himself and
us all." Much may be done by personal endeavour guided
with patience, forbearance, and good temper, towards forwarding the knowledge of the Native gardeners, but it is a
long tiresome and tedious road, is there not a shorter ?—